PARENTING
IN THE
AGE OF FACEBOOK

Marzia Hassan (LLB, MSW, RSW), who began her career as a corporate lawyer, started work as a social worker and relationship consultant with individuals, couples and families after a decade of self-driven learning and professional study. She runs Family Connections International, a psychotherapy practice based in Toronto; facilitates parenting, self-development and spiritual learning groups; and, in recent years, has conducted online parenting workshops. As a relationship expert, Marzia has featured on television, across South Asian magazines, and has been honoured by the Canadian House of Commons. Marzia, a mother of three, lives in Toronto.

PARENTING
IN THE
AGE OF FACEBOOK

Raising the Net Generation

MARZIA HASSAN

RUPA

Published by
Rupa Publications India Pvt. Ltd 2016
7/16, Ansari Road, Daryaganj
New Delhi 110002

Sales centres:
Allahabad Bengaluru Chennai
Hyderabad Jaipur Kathmandu
Kolkata Mumbai

ISBN: 978-81-291-3773-9

First impression 2016

10 9 8 7 6 5 4 3 2 1

The moral right of the author has been asserted.

Typeset by SÜRYA, New Delhi

Printed at HT Media Ltd., Noida

Dedicated to

My parents for believing in me

*My parenting partner and cheerleader, Muslim,
for being the rock in our family*

*My children Sara, Zehra and Sadiq for being (mostly) willing
subjects to the many parenting experiments and giving me
feedback on what worked (and what didn't)
You guys make it all worthwhile*

Contents

Part 1

FACING REALITY

Chapter 1

Exploring the Digital Landscape

We shape our tools and afterwards our tools shape us.
—Marshall McLuhan

I am not an expert on social media or the Internet. I am not a computer whizz. My children, like most of their peers, are far ahead of me in technology and while I struggle to understand and navigate the digital landscape, it comes naturally to them. So why am I writing a book on raising the Net Generation—or, raising kids in the age of Facebook?

Because I am a parent, like you, whose parenting world changed pretty much overnight.

I adopted technology early. It was at my university in the 1980s that I made the switch from my electronic typewriter to the Apple Macintosh computer. It was a happy day. No longer did I have to laboriously correct mistakes by hitting backspace on the typewriter and whiting it out. I could be much more productive. I could type faster without having to worry about correcting mistakes or checking spellings as I went along (always a tedious task for me).

When my husband and I began a family in the early 1990s, we enthusiastically brought a personal computer home and eagerly started using it. The computer, like the TV, was in a public place and the entire family shared its use. As in the old days when the single family television was the only screen in the house, the use of the computer was shared by the entire family. This meant that it was not available at all times to everyone. Computer time, like TV time, had a clear beginning and end.

You watched TV and then you went on with your real life. You went on the computer to check email, do your homework, play a game or two, and then you went about the rest of your day. The lines of when 'computer time' for any member of the family began and ended were clear.

The children were curious and wanted to play on this new machine—exciting new software and games enticed both them and me. Even then, I was adamant that computer time, like TV time, was strictly rationed so that the children could engage in a broad range of activities which fed their mind, body and soul. Instinctively, we knew not to leave children unsupervised on the computer, just as we would not leave them unsupervised in a public playground. In the early days of the Internet and technology, it did not appear as a threat to family life or to the children's well-being. Although it was attractive and the children begged to be allowed to use it more and more, we could control its use and impact by controlling their access to it.

Sharing the computer as a family taught us many lessons in sharing, rationing, being considerate and, at some level, knowing that it was a precious resource to be used mindfully—that if anyone overstepped its use, there would be consequences, both in terms of total time allotted and the impact on relationships in the family.

Even so, there were signs to show that parents needed to acquire a different kind of vigilance in this virtual playground. Alia, a parent in one of my early parenting groups, recalls how she became aware of the dangers in a rather dramatic fashion. She said, 'One day, I was using the drop-down menu in the browsing history to find a site I had visited the previous day and, to my horror, I found a couple of adult pornography sites in the browsing history. My heart sank. The only other person at that time using the family computer was my pre-adolescent son. He seemed so innocent. Could I be so wrong about his sexual maturity? Had I misjudged his innocence and his nature? I thought he reported everything to me.

'Normally, I would have waited and planned a strategy in a situation like this, but I was so distressed that I called him immediately and showed him what I had found. "Help me understand this," I said. He burst into tears and explained that a group of lads at his school had sent these sites to the whole class. They had announced that they would be sending some porn out. Not knowing what porn was, my son thought that it was "pawn", as in a chess piece. He was obviously traumatized by what he had seen and I felt dismayed that my child had been exposed to something he was obviously not prepared for. Because I was mostly at home and my children were young and fairly innocent, it had not occurred to me to put any kind of blocks or filters on the family computer.'

Sadly, this was not the only instance of the potential negative power of the Internet brought up in the parenting group. Smita talked about her children's first pet, a rabbit. 'They excitedly brought it home and wanted to become experts on looking after it. By this time, Google was already establishing itself as the source of all information on the planet. So they googled "Taking care of your bunny"—but all sorts of pornographic images started popping up. What was a completely innocent search by young children turned into a traumatic experience! Horrified, they pulled the plug from the computer, completely confused.'

Since then, talking to countless groups of parents about the impact of digital technology on the family, I have keenly become aware that worse things could happen.

The next big shift came with mobile technology. In pre-mobile technology days, the standard advice I would give parents was to have a shared family computer, to put it in a public place and make sure that parents were around when children were online. This advice was relatively easy for parents to digest as they had grown up in an age where media had been a shared family activity. Even for affluent families, it was common to have one television set which was in the 'TV lounge', around which the family gathered each night. Despite occasional protests that no one was talking to each other, the family members were all in the same room and focused on the same programme, which meant they had a shared experience they could talk about or discuss later.

The situation has significantly changed since the mobile age. Now there is no clear line between online time and offline time as our devices are always with us and we switch or toggle between real life and virtual life, being physically present for those in the room while emotionally and mentally connecting to others who are in virtual space.

What has stood out for me while talking to parents over the years is how many otherwise conscious parents, who take the responsibility of parenting very seriously and who are in charge of their families, feel ill-equipped to deal with the issues of technology and its appropriate use in the home. Highly educated, professional and competent parents report that their children are so far ahead of them in accessing and using technology that they are unsure of what to do. These parents are not to blame. Every community has certain norms that it expects its members to follow. People are expected to behave in certain ways in public spaces. How are we to react, then, when all social norms and etiquette are currently in flux? Whether one is standing in line at a supermarket, in a doctor's office, at a religious sermon or a funeral, there are people speaking on cell phones, texting, checking emails and sending messages. How do we decide what is acceptable behaviour and what is not, especially when most people around us seem to see nothing wrong with it? How are we to train our children in pro-social behaviour when the boundaries of what constitutes it are no longer agreed on?

So many parents I spoke to threw up their hands in despair, either because they were unaware of the pitfalls of letting their children roam freely on the worldwide web or because they were not active users of digital technology and, therefore, felt ill-equipped to handle it. At other times, parents thought they had educated themselves and installed what they felt were safety features and yet, they were caught unawares because something new had come up. It is clear that changes are occurring very fast. The Internet age is still in its infancy. Many parents find it greatly challenging to stay on top of technology and feel overwhelmed at how it appears to have taken hold of their families, eating into family time and relationships and changing the way that families communicate.

And yet, there are some experts who believe that nothing has really changed.[1] They claim that children are who they have always been, curious, wanting to connect with their peers, resisting parental authority, discovering their identity and being creative. It is only the platform on which they engage that is different. And parents have always been suspicious of children, so that's not new.

The assertion that nothing much has changed goes against what parents experience every day as they compare their own childhood to the world inhabited by their children. So let us look at how the parenting and family landscape has irrevocably and completely changed. Not all the changes are bad. Many families find that technology is bringing them closer to loved ones who live far away. Others remark that it has made life easier in many ways, especially for access to information. Most parents concur, however, that despite its good effects, technology is impacting their families in ways that are not always healthy. They worry that their children are so entrenched in the virtual world that they are not living life in real time, face-to-face with other human beings. Although research is being done on the various effects of technology on the family, I believe that the full impact of the unbridled adoption and use of technology will not be known for some time. By then, it may be too late for a whole generation of young people.

Exploring the new family landscape

1) Time: the way we spend our time, both at work and leisure, has dramatically changed. There is no clear division between work and leisure as our work comes home with us and we can snatch moments of leisure while we are working by visiting social media and other websites.

2) Attention: now we divide our attention between several tasks at the same time. We are continuously tethered to our various devices while we try to manage our real-time obligations.

3) Digital footprints: the hallmark of the Internet is that once something is 'posted' on the Internet, it stays there forever. The person who initially posted it has no control over it.

4) Communication:

   a. In pre-Internet days, communication was generally between two people. You could prevent people from overhearing by making sure there was no one around or you could whisper. Now, once you put something online on a public platform, such as a social networking site (SNS), you have no idea who will witness your communication. In fact, everything that you put on a social media site is public by default. Since the nature of social networking sites is to encourage sharing and public broadcasting, whatever you share will be public unless you take intentional steps to limit it. Reflecting on where and how your communication may potentially end up requires great foresight and self-control, which the quickness of the Internet actually discourages.

b. You can communicate with people at a distance, often at the expense of those who are close. Paradoxically, even though the audience for a given piece of information is potentially unlimited, the act of going online and communicating is essentially an individualistic activity and has the potential to cut you off from those in the same geographical location, but connect you to those who are remote.

c. Digital communication is mostly via text rather than voice. Even communication between two people needs skills and forethought as you need to decode text and written language without the benefit of tone, body language or facial expression. Since words have been touted as being only 7 per cent of communication, the Net Generation needs new kinds of skills to decode that 7 per cent.

d. Communication is asynchronistic—a conversation via text or instant messaging does not have a clear beginning and end, as it is on the telephone or face-to-face. Potentially, one can have a conversation which stretches over several hours or days.

5) You can search for information at the press of a button. In the digital age, no one needs to ponder over a question. The moment a question arises in our heads, we can google it for an answer. The Internet has democratized information—both scholars and students have access to the same information. Although knowledge is accessible to

a wider audience than ever before, it can encourage breadth of information at the expense of depth of thought, which requires reflection and contemplation.

6) Sharing of information via the Internet is effortless and fast. It has a very low investment time, which encourages the recipient of information to pass it forward. So any piece of information on the Internet can be shared with an endlessly growing audience. Additionally, the social media and other websites greatly encourage this forwarding of information as it means additional or potential customers, increasing the bottom line in terms of profit.

Let us consider a few issues of further concern for parents:

1) The pace of change has been at lightning speed. Many parents don't know what hit them. Before parents are alerted and soon after their child is introduced to a digital device, the toddler has turned into a technology-addicted zombie who cannot be prised away from the screen.

2) This is the first generation of children who surpass their parents in knowledge and skill-sets at a very young age. Earlier, children asked parents questions, but now they can google those questions. Of course, the answers will very likely be devoid of context or shared family values, which means that parents have much less influence over their young children's minds, hearts and souls than in previous generations. Parents have always mentored, trained and educated their offspring in life skills and in the ways of the world, but the Net Generation born into a digital world learn to navigate it instinctively and are vastly more tech-savvy than their parents, turning the balance of knowledge upside down very early on.

3) Keeping children safe has taken on a whole new meaning.

Previous generations knew their children were safe and protected when they were home. Even though children needed to be taught skills to stay safe, they were cocooned from the 'big bad world'. For the Net Generation, the big bad world has invaded family living rooms, kitchens and even nurseries. While parents would not allow young children to go into the street or town unsupervised and without safety training and measures in place, many children today are roaming the virtual world without any fence or boundary.

Since we are the first generation of parents to deal with this situation, we do not have the wisdom of historical perspective. Perhaps for the first time in human history, the young are ahead of older people and need them less and less for learning, companionship and advice. This is uncharted territory and it is no surprise if we find ourselves out of our depth.

In praise of Web 2.0

It needs to be said at the very outset that this book is not a rant against technology. There is much to praise digital technology for. It has the potential to add value to our lives, to allow us to bridge geographical limitations and help us be a closer part of each other's lives. Here are some positive ways it has impacted family life and parenting, as shared by various parents in our group.

Making the world smaller and keeping in touch

'When I left home for university, the only way to keep in touch with my parents was through letters or an expensive telephone call. With the advent of the Internet and digital technology, we can now keep in touch frequently and cheaply with our children, who are currently away at university.'

'Our extended family is becoming increasingly mobile and moving in search of greener economic pastures and safer communities, and today, we are spread over a greater geographical area. It is much easier for us to stay in regular contact with each other and be a part of each other's lives, despite the geographical distance.'

'As a new grandparent, I rely on Skype to connect daily with my grandchildren and to share their growth milestones. I am not well enough to travel to see them, so I am very grateful that we have a good Skype connection.'

'Once the children left home for university, WhatsApp became our lifeline. We use it to check in with each other, to inform each other of our whereabouts and to share pictures and memories when we are travelling.'

'We can get the best deals and check out places before we get there. We never go to a hotel without checking it out on TripAdvisor. It tells us how family-friendly the place is and what facilities are available for children.'

'As a parent with young children, the Internet allows me to work remotely from home. This means that I take fewer days off when my kids are sick. Working virtually also allows me to save on costs related to travel for work, clothes and so on.'

Virtual communities as a support system

'I am a part of online parenting groups. I find online forums and groups are extraordinarily generous when it comes to sharing information, support and advice on many different parenting issues. Virtual communities have been very helpful in giving me parenting advice and support. No matter what the issue one is dealing with, there always seems to be an online forum or a blog relating to that issue that can offer support and suggestions.'

'After the actual parenting group is over, I like to extend the learning experience and continue the conversation through a virtual parenting group. I find the ongoing support very beneficial and I have also invited other parents to join. There, the parents are able to share stories and provide ongoing support to each other. I have developed friendships with several of the participants, have messaged them privately and even met a couple of them.'

'I am no longer stuck when my children ask me questions I do not know the answer to. I frequently google to answer their questions.'

'Our family uses social media to raise awareness about social issues that we are passionate about. We realized the power of social media in the recent mass-scale demonstrations in Paris, the likes of which the world has not seen before. My teenage children also use Twitter to keep big businesses accountable. When they have a bad experience at a restaurant or an airline, for example, they Tweet it to their friends who in turn pass it on. They really feel empowered for they do not have to accept poor service or a substandard product merely because they are young. The companies they Tweet about usually get in touch with them to make things right, because they know the power of social media. I wish I had that kind of power over large businesses when I was young.'

'I grew up in a remote town in Belgium with few people from my faith and community. As a result, my parents found it hard to provide me with language skills and religious education. As an adult, I feel that I really missed out on learning about my heritage. I am extremely grateful for the Internet now because I can teach my own children our language and about our religion. Also, they can now form virtual communities with those who are struggling with similar cultural and religious issues. As a result, my children are much more religiously and culturally aware than I was at their age.'

Talking to all these parents, it was clear that the benefits of

Internet support the active parenting that they are already doing, although they are not a replacement for parenting or for family time. And here lies the test of whether something is beneficial or not. If the tools of technology are replacing human contact, if they are taking time away from family or other important activities, they need to be managed better. If they actually contribute beneficially to real life, they are inherently valuable tools that will enhance family life and parenting, but the tools should not dominate us.

A significant portion of this book is devoted to exploring the impact of technology on various aspects of our children's and families' lives. Many studies and much research is quoted and some of it may seem horrifying to parents. The intention is not to scare you or predict the worst-case scenario regarding technology. The purpose is to inform you regarding potential issues with the wholesale and unconscious adoption of all things tech. I believe we can only prepare ourselves when we know what we are up against. It is very tempting indeed, to bury our heads, ostrich-like, and hope that all will be okay. In this day and age, unfortunately, that is not an option. Our children are the first generation of digital natives and by the time technology's full impact on their lives becomes clear, it will be too late. We need to arm ourselves with knowledge of the pitfalls so that we can guide and train our children to be safe from the ill effects of the misuse of technology while, at the same time, encourage them to explore its many beneficial facets. By doing this, we can ensure that they are healthy, successful and mindful users of technology, effective digital citizens of a world where real and virtual lives run parallel to each other and are impacted by each other.

In much of the research available, there is a consistent and disturbing trend: parents are consistently underestimating the risks that their own children have been exposed to. In the EU

(European) Kids Online Study, for example, 40 per cent of parents whose children had been exposed to sexual images said that their children had not been exposed to any pornography, 56 per cent of parents whose child had been bullied online said that their child had not, and 61 per cent of parents whose child had met someone in person after communicating with them online said that their child had never met an online contact in person.[2]

It seems that our generation of parents is in denial about what our children are doing online and the kinds of risks that they are exposed to. It is imperative that we wake up to the reality and face facts.

Secondly, in order to prepare the Net Generation, we, as parents, need to look at our own relationship with technology. Many parents in the groups wailed that the Internet had taken over their lives and that family life had suffered as a result. Some admitted to being addicted to the Internet themselves while trying to control the children. It started to become increasingly clear that managing technology was a family issue as much as it was a parenting one. While parents definitely need to establish good habits, set limits and impose positive discipline in the sphere of technology, they should also look at their own tech habits and consider what model they present to their children.

After informing ourselves about the impact of technology and looking at our own relationship with it, we need to develop parenting practices that are based on sound principles and that can be applied to managing technology in the home. In a sense, although the landscape of parenting has changed, the compass of good instinct and conscious parenting still works and a good map (or navigation system) will still help you get there. The aim of this book is to help you fine-tune your internal compass (of good instinct), to help you pay attention to what is working and what is not with regard to your family's interaction with technology, and to provide you with a road map of parenting practices to navigate this new landscape.

In terms of dealing with issues, it seems about 50 per cent of parents are doing it reactively.[3] Parents are monitoring use and restricting Internet access as a means of punishing children. Punishing children by taking away technology is not effective in most instances, as many parents who have tried it will attest. Such measures are usually taken when anger is the trigger or when we react negatively, so it will do little to teach children skills that foster a mindful relationship with technology. What is more effective is providing support, educating and training ourselves and our children about Internet safety, making rules thoughtfully and with consultation, and using teaching moments. Sound parenting practices like these require more effort upfront but have the potential to train our children and ourselves to become sensible digital citizens and use technology as part of a balanced, healthy lifestyle.

As parents, we need to adopt new factors mindfully and cautiously, to try them out and see if they make family life better or are taking it in a direction that goes against our values. It is for these reasons that I espouse a balanced but firm approach in this book. It is not a tirade against the evils of technology, about how it has spoilt some mythical, utopian past. The age of technology, as far as we can tell, is here to stay. There is no looking back. If we choose to barricade ourselves from its influence, it will be an uphill battle *and* is not realistic for most of us. Most of us want our children to be active contributing members of the global village, citizens of the world, so to speak. In order to raise the Net Generation to be good digital citizens of this global world, we need to confront reality, assess our children's use of technology, inform ourselves about the impact of its use, and to practise parenting in a way that supports our goal of raising digital citizens in harmony with their world.

Chapter 2

What Are Your Children Doing Online?

Surely a long life must be somewhat tedious, since we are forced to
call in so many trifling things to help rid us of our time,
which will never return.
—Samuel Johnson

Aasiya was tearful when she walked into my office. 'The worst thing is,' she started before she even sat down, 'that I do not know what my children are doing online. I am continuously nagging them to get off their laptops. The more I nag, the more they ignore me. Every interaction on this subject seems to be full of conflict. I've had it!'

A mother of four children between the ages of nine and sixteen, Aasiya clearly had her hands full. 'I used to be quite in control when the children were younger,' she continued. 'I was careful about what they did, what they watched on TV and for how long. My eldest was almost a teenager before he started going online by himself. Then things started to go downhill,' she said. 'When I went back to work after my youngest child started middle school, I became a bit more lenient about how much time they spent on the computer. Once the smartphone came into the house, however, it has never been the same.' With less time on her hands and with the growing influence of the children's peers, she and her husband Amar gave in to the oldest son Salim's demand for a smartphone. 'I felt it was a bad idea at the time, but I could not articulate why and had too many things going on at the time to think things through.'

Many parents might relate to Aasiya's experience. In many households, the first step to digital technology is taken without much thought or discussion. It is driven more by what is within the family budget and which model to get than a consideration of the impact it will have on the family, especially the children, and on the parenting relationship.

Few parents can say exactly when it dawned on them, when the light bulb went on, that matters were getting out of control. Parents describe it more as a growing sense of unease, that something in their family was not quite right, but they were not sure what. By the time they realized that digital technology was taking over their lives, they felt that it was too late. By this time, the situation had become so entrenched that it was very hard to change.

If you are among those parents, know that this is the problem with digital technology. It is the nature of the beast, so to speak. It starts innocently enough. A child (or a parent) gets an iPad or a new smartphone and there is much excitement. The family excitedly explores the many wonders the gadget can do. The owner of the new gadget, be it parent or child, starts to depend upon it increasingly and soon it becomes more than a habit, a necessity of sorts. It becomes the first thing to connect with in the morning and the last at night. Parents also remark that the time spent on the Internet seems to make their children retreat into their own worlds. Parents, at least those who do not have addiction issues of their own, cannot understand what is so attractive about spending most of one's waking time staring into a screen and typing on a flat, touch-sensitive keyboard. Much too often, once technology comes into the home without a plan of how to manage it, its use tends to spill over into family life. It becomes a source of conflict and parents become concerned about their children's virtual lives.

Most parents will not be surprised to learn that Internet use amongst children is currently both deepening and broadening—

more and more children are accessing the Internet and are doing so for a longer period of time. According to one survey, 80 per cent of middle and high income families reported having a smartphone and 65 per cent of the same group owned a tablet.[1]

The greatest increase in use over the last two years has been among children under nine years of age, while the amount of use has increased across all age groups in children under eighteen.[2] Studies also show that parents tend to be somewhat careful when it comes to very young children being unsupervised on the Internet, but this drops off at an early stage. Parents report that children start using digital devices independently as early as six years old.[3]

At the same time as online access and use for children is growing, it seems that parental monitoring of children's online activity is on the decline. The Digital Futures study by Jeffery Cole, for the University of Southern California, found that the percentage of parents monitoring their children on SNSs has gone down in the last few years.[4] Parents said that they trusted their children online and saw no reason to monitor them, or they believed that doing so would show a lack of trust in them. Of those who do monitor their children, only half the parents have password access to their children's social media accounts.[5]

Studies show that many parents do recognize that there is potential danger in unrestricted access to technology.[6] At the same time, more than 30 per cent of parents today, according to the Digital Futures report, say that their children spend too much time on the Internet.[7] It appears that even though parents realize that children are engaging in something harmful, they feel powerless to control it.

Research also shows that many parents are either unaware or in denial about how much time their children are spending on the Internet, while 40 per cent of parents believe that children, in general, spend too much time on their devices and that this might impact time spent with the family. Surprisingly though, only 18 per cent of parents believe that it is *their* children who are spending too much time on digital technology.[8] So, they generally underestimate the amount of time their offspring are roaming unsupervised in digital playgrounds. Given that many children over the age of ten (and some under) have access to smartphones and tablets, this is not surprising. Unlike a television set or a desktop computer, which is often in a public part of the house, mobile technology by definition is portable and its use private. Additionally, if you account for the fact that many Net Gens are frequently using multiple platforms and apps at the same time, the issue becomes compounded. Often, users themselves are not aware of how much time they are spending on their own devices and tend to underestimate it.

When parents are asked about their concerns about excess technology use impacting their children's well-being, it seems that the top two concerns are about lack of exercise (59 per cent of parents) and privacy online with the lurking danger of predators (53 per cent).[9] While these are two important aspects of healthy technology use, it does not even begin to cover all the potential impacts on children's well-being.

What this study also found was that the amount and quality of tech use in the home was often a cause of conflict, but that few parents had clear rules for it. Rather, the use of technology was managed on a case-by-case basis.[10] When questioned about this, parents usually cite the rapid pace of change, the sheer number of devices with mind-boggling capabilities, and not recognizing the impact that the device was going to have on their lives until it was too late.

Although some parents report being media savvy, they do

not interact with and use media in the same way as watching TV together with the children, reading a book, or watching sports or a play. It seems that while parents prefer older media, children are more attracted to newer media, a lot of which is either a sole activity or an entirely peer-focused one.[11] Older research on TV watching suggests that children learn more from TV in the company of parents who comment on and coach throughout the programme; but today, solo viewing of media is compromising our children's ability to learn from educational material.

It is important to understand what children are doing online and how it impacts them. Part 2 of this book delves into the impact of online access on children. We must understand the impact for two reasons: firstly, information is power. If we understand the full impact of what our children's digital diet is doing to them, we will be more motivated to take appropriate action. We may also recognize that we are focusing on the wrong aspect and can then direct our efforts to winning the battle by improving our strategy. Secondly, it also helps us to talk to our children in an informed way. Very often, when we react from fear rather than knowledge, it misses the mark with our children because it does not match their lived reality. If we actually know what we are talking about, backing it up with facts and figures, we can get greater leverage with our children.

Meanwhile, the way the Net Generation uses technology is also changing. In a 2010 study, most teens accessed their computers and devices to play video games.[12] In the most recent survey, it seems that visiting social networks has become the most popular activity among children aged eight to eighteen.[13]

It needs to be said that not all online activity is the same and not every use of digital technology needs to cause parents concern. In interviews with various groups of parents, three top concerns centred on:

1) What information do children access?
2) Who are they connecting to?
3) How do they behave?

Let us try and understand what the Net Generation is doing when they are online.

Looking for information, recreation and connections

The Net Generation uses the Internet for learning as well as for recreation. For many children, the Internet is their first (and often only) stop for gathering information. Many schools encourage children even before grade 1 to use the Internet to do simple searches. Research for homework online is entirely acceptable and, in fact, encouraged by many schools. This can be very convenient and fast if children are taught to distinguish reliable information from unreliable websites. Over time, it appears that some children may become more savvy about the reliability of information accessed via the Internet, although this is a topic that needs to be addressed from the very first time that they access information online. Many schools are increasingly turning to posting information about classes and relevant reading materials online. This is, of course, highly convenient, inexpensive and an environmentally conscious choice.

It is interesting that a vast majority of children under twelve (89 per cent) believe that most of the information available online is trustworthy and they consider themselves to be savvy consumers of technology. Although a significant proportion of children have been victims of misinformation, they continue to trust the Internet. In fact, a significant proportion of children rated the Internet, including Wikipedia, as a more reliable source of information for school projects than published books. Even children as young as eleven years old report being more Internet-savvy than their peers. Although children younger than twelve agree that their parents are a more reliable source of information than the Internet, this gap narrows quickly for children over twelve years old. This is worrying and shows that parents and educators should train children to decipher credible information.[14]

In terms of non-school-related access for entertainment purposes, children use the Internet in the following ways:

They use it to connect with friends, both real-life and online, through SNS: the Internet is the average child's social lifeline. It is the equivalent of hanging out with friends after school, going to the canteen/coffee shop, friends' houses, sleepovers and other such activities. Children can stay in touch with many friends at the same time by posting public messages on SNSs, such as Facebook, or they can send private messages. They can share pictures and videos that they have created or that appeal to them; they can also play online games with real-life or Facebook friends.

There are, however, significant differences in how children and adults use Facebook and other SNSs. Whereas adults are more likely to use them to keep in touch with real-life friends, children use them to broadcast incidents in their life, to gather as many friends and 'likes' as they can, to boost social capital.[15]

Children also use other online methods to stay in touch with friends, such as texting or instant messaging, and not always by means of the written word. Youth today communicate as much, if not more, by sharing pictures and videos as they do by written messages.[16] This explains the popularity of apps such as Snapchat, Instagram, and WhatsApp, all of which allow the seamless sharing of pictures.

Some children are also making new friends online. The Norton study found that 35 per cent of children under eighteen had online friends whom they had never met in person[17], whereas an EU study in twenty-five countries of 25,000 parents and children found that 40 per cent of children had found new friends online.[18]

They create, share and view videos and other content. YouTube, a site for watching and sharing videos, is currently one of the most popular websites on the Internet. Both adults and children enjoy watching entertaining and educational videos. However, unlike the digital immigrants, the Net Generation are not passive consumers of digital media, but actively participate in creating and uploading content as much as in viewing other people's content. And even though adults participate in these worlds, they are on an unequal footing with the younger ones. Neither age, nor educational level, nor life experience gives them an edge over their younger, more digitally adept counterparts and, in this way, the Internet is the most democratic of spaces, erasing the traditional measures of status and power.

According to a recent study from the Pew Internet & American Life project, more than 50 per cent of the Net Generation have created media content, and about 30 per cent have shared the content they created.[19] So, unlike the digital immigrants, the Digital Natives are active participants, creating, sharing and co-creating their virtual reality. The Net Generation, perhaps more than other generations before them, are interactively shaping their own culture.

They are using it for good: the Net Generation has immense power through social media broadcasting and for keeping corporate and political powers accountable. They do not suffer in silence. If 'dissed', they will take their case to the worldwide web and inform their peers, who in turn will broadcast widely. A single Tweet or Facebook post has the ability to get noticed by businesses and organizations which in turn upgrade their customer service policies.

The reality that children are both consuming information and producing and sharing ideas and artistic expression on the Internet means that there is an urgent need for their cognitive skills and judgement to develop so that they can decipher what should be shared or not. Moreover, parents need to pay special attention to strengthening the foundation of values for children, so that they create and consume content on firm values and morals.

They are shopping: according to the Norton Online Living Report, which surveyed approximately 2,700 children under the age of eighteen in eight countries, between 35 per cent (USA) to 69 per cent (China) of children report being confident shoppers online. Since it is often easier to buy at the click of a button, targeting of children as potential customers is particularly worrying for parents who may not want their children to shop online for a variety of reasons.[20]

They visit virtual worlds and play video-based games: virtual worlds are online environments where users can play with other online users using a virtual self, or an avatar, which they can design themselves. There is much debate on the validity of virtual worlds and online games to develop a child's imagination.[21] Elizabeth Stutz, who is actively against video games and online worlds, argues that left to their own imaginations and some space, indoors or out, children craft their own worlds; they find themselves and gain confidence through their interactions with fellow playmates; and act out issues and stresses in their life through play-acting to gain emotional mastery.[22] On the other end of the spectrum, proponents of video games, such as James Newman, claim that online games are not restrictive and help users explore and define their virtual worlds in a unique way.[23]

Yet others argue that it is no longer possible to distinguish between virtual and real worlds because the two meld together so seamlessly, and that children's abilities to construct and use avatars allow them to experiment with social identity in less risky ways than in real life.[24]

So, to summarize the answer to parents' questions about what is so attractive about 'going online', either through a smartphone, a tablet or computer, is that technology fulfils many needs. It is so multi-functional. A phone is not simply devised to answer calls and text messages. It holds the key to many of our daily issues, such as giving us company and solace when we are alone. Mr Google knows more than any parent, and provides entertainment as well as companionship, information and organization.

And therein lies the issue. Although we have used gadgets and gizmos, they never fulfilled such a range of human needs as mobile technology does today. Given that it appears to be all things to many people, it is not surprising that adults and children are attracted to it and it is very unlikely that we can control access to technology for any length of time. Hope for us lies in being able to embrace it in a wholesome manner and use it rather than be used by it.

This book is not an unconditional and resigned acceptance of all things technological in the home, nor does it recommend rejection of all things technical. Instead, it offers insights into the pros and cons of the various aspects of technology and invites fellow parents to adopt each new device cautiously and with conscious choice, setting rules and boundaries, and seeing how these work in the short and long term. Given the nature of technology and its wide-ranging impact on every aspect of our lives, the steps we take as parents today to manage it in our own lives and in the lives of our children will have an impact on their future. As in other aspects of parenting, we do not and cannot expect young children to know what is good for them or to figure out things by trial and error. It is our job as parents and we need to take it seriously.

Summary of what you should know

- ❐ A very high percentage of children have access to the Internet, in their homes, schools and public places.
- ❐ Internet access is on the rise in all parts of the world.
- ❐ Internet use increases with age—older children and adults use it more than children.
- ❐ Children are starting to use the Internet at younger ages than even a few years ago.
- ❐ Children are spending more time on the Internet than they did even a few years ago.
- ❐ Parents generally try to control access for very young children, but become increasingly lax as children grow up slightly.
- ❐ Most parents are not setting limits for Internet use in their homes.
- ❐ Parents are generally unaware about the impact of an unbridled use of technology on their children.

Part 2

ASSESSING THE IMPACT OF TECHNOLOGY

Chapter 3

Impact on the Brain

I'm not really one for reading books. I have a very poor attention span. I'd rather listen to music, play games or watch films on my iPad.
—Olly Murs

I recently found myself waiting for a hotel elevator with a family that consisted of a mother, a father, a daughter aged about thirteen and a son aged nine. As we waited, the children were glued to their iPads, completely oblivious to their surroundings. The son did not miss a beat while his dad put things into his backpack. After he was done, he put the backpack onto the shoulders of his young son by guiding his arms into the spot for the shoulder strap, and tightened it slightly so that it would fit comfortably. When the elevator came, he guided his son in and pressed the button. Then, when the elevator opened out to the lobby floor, he led his son out and gently pressed his shoulders to indicate the right direction. I watched in fascination at this scene being played out.

We walked out together and as we were in the line waiting for a taxi, I struck up a conversation with the parents and explained that I was writing a book on parenting in the digital age and asked if they would be willing to talk to me.

We met later that evening over coffee and I began by asking if it was typical for the kids to be glued to their screens while they were in a public place and how life was like at home.

'Pretty much the same,' said Priti, a well-groomed and intelligent young woman. 'My son has been very interested in computers and programming since a very young age. We have no real reason to stop him,' she explained. 'He gets very good grades and is generally well behaved.' I asked her if she was concerned about attention or addiction issues stemming from so much time spent on devices. She replied that, in fact, he used to be hyperactive as a child, which caused concern, but they soon discovered that being onscreen actually helps him focus. 'My in-laws do tell me that he is addicted but I don't think they understand that this is the way the new generation is.'

Attention issues

It is not unusual for mothers like Priti to disagree with in-laws on this issue. There is a raging debate among parents, teachers and technology experts on whether or not digital technologies have caused children's attention spans to shorten, or if spending endless time on devices constitutes addiction.

Psychologists define the attention span as 'the amount of time we can focus on a task before we start to "zone out".' Teachers and parents complain that children today spend a shorter amount of time focused on a single task or object. Some studies suggest that the average attention span of an American adult has shrunk from twelve minutes a mere decade ago to about five minutes today.[1] While it is difficult to conduct similar studies on children, this decrease suggests an alarming trend.

Many teachers believe that today's classrooms are more challenging because children cannot focus on a task for too long. The Pew Research Center in the USA surveyed about 2,500 teachers and found that the vast majority (87 per cent) believed that digital technology has resulted in a generation of children that is 'easily distracted with short attention spans'. Almost two-thirds of these teachers (64 per cent) also found that digital technologies and constant access to them 'do more to distract students than to help them academically'.[2]

Although scientists have been reluctant to confirm a casual link between technology and the shortened attention span, it is clear that today there is both more screen time spent by young kids *and* more diagnoses of attention disorders.

Among common attention issues exhibited by children today are the constellation of symptoms known as Attention Deficit Disorder (ADD) or Attention Deficit Hyperactivity Disorder (ADHD). ADHD is a neurobehavioural developmental disorder. Children diagnosed with ADD or ADHD have trouble staying focused on a task, they are restless, fidgety, have poor impulse control and are easily angered, sometimes even destroying property. Parents describe these children as hyperactive and are often frustrated because they get into trouble at school for being disruptive. The diagnoses of ADD and ADHD have increased more than 40 per cent in less than a decade and according to the Center for Disease Control in the USA, about 11 per cent of all young people in America suffer from ADD, making it the most common psychiatric disorder.[3]

The fact that ADHD has become a common diagnosis for children today does not mitigate the child's suffering, nor is it any comfort to the parents who often experience a great deal of frustration and guilt because they feel that they cannot control their child.

While there may be other factors contributing to the rise in ADHD, such as nutrition, genetics and the environment, it is generally accepted that spending long periods in front of a screen is significant because it keeps the brain hyper-stimulated for prolonged periods of time. Like Priti, many parents are likely to put hyperactive kids in front of a screen to calm them down because they appear to be able to focus on screens more than on any other thing. One reason why children pay attention easily to video games is because of the intermittent rewards provided by a game. When they take an action required by the game, they are rewarded through points or move up a level. When this happens, the brain releases dopamine, the feel-good neurotransmitter that activates the pleasure centres in the brain and makes them feel good. So what looks likes focused attention to the parent is, in fact, a cycle created by this intermittent reward inherent in the video game. Conversely, it is likely to perpetuate the cycle of hyperactivity in the long run.

According to a study published in the *Journal of Pediatrics*, children in elementary and middle schools who spend more than two hours a day in front of screens, whether it is playing video games or watching TV, are about twice as likely to suffer from attention issues.[4] Attention issues were also found in college students who had prolonged exposure to digital media. Experts, such as Dr Dimitri Christakis, director of the Child Health Institute at the University of Washington in Seattle, believe that digital media and screen time have adverse effects on attention spans in both children and adults. He says that the younger the child is at the age of exposure the greater the risk of attention-related issues. His research found that the youngest children are the most vulnerable to the detrimental impact of digital media on attention—every hour that children are exposed to televisions and other screens from the ages of one to three raises the risk of them having attention problems by age seven by almost 10 per cent. He also found that kids under the age of five who watched two hours of TV a day were 20 per cent more likely than kids who watched no TV to have attention problems at the school age.[5]

Other researchers have found a similar link. Larry Rosen and his colleagues at California State University found a link between technology use and attention problems in four- to eight-year-olds. For nine- to twelve-year-olds, the use of video games specifically increased attention problems, while for teenagers, media use, online gaming, video games and online time predicted both behaviour problems and attention issues.[6] Technology-related attention issues have become such a concern that they have been given the name of Technology-related Attention Deficit Disorder (T-ADD).[7]

Additionally, when a child's mind is continuously exposed to the fast-changing and stimulating environment of the digital world, real life and school become slow, colourless and boring in comparison, making it harder for children to focus on them. This is especially troubling because by its very nature, schooling needs to inculcate basic skills and knowledge that may not be immediately entertaining or exciting but which are essential to further learning. Schools today face an uphill battle in making academics fun and engaging to the Net Generation. In every worthwhile pursuit, sheer persistence and plodding is necessary to get through a specific learning hurdle. These valuable life skills appear to be much harder for the Net Generation to master as their brains become increasingly used to the rush of novelty and stimulation provided by digital technology.

Hyperactive children with attention-related issues frequently have poor emotional regulation, which means that they may have trouble making friends and are ostracized by their peers. They have an easier time making friends online, since their online peers do not have to deal with the full package of energy that these children exude. Turning to screens and technology to address these issues may provide the parents a brief respite but, in the long term, these tactics only serve to exacerbate attention issues.

Addiction

Onlookers observing young Amit on his iPad noticed that he was so addicted to his device that he could not take his attention away from it, regardless of what was happening in his environment. Several parents during interviews for this book asked if the amount of time their children spent on their devices was normal or if they were addicted.

Whether or not technology addiction is real is a hotly debated subject.[8] Psychologists who believe that technology, like drugs or gambling, can be addictive explain that the same neurotransmitter dopamine, which causes addictive behaviour may be at play here. Dopamine activity in the brain feels good because it activates the pleasure centres of the brain, which is the neurological reason why children and adolescents seek online video games. When a child becomes thus trained to pay attention because of the rewards, it not only makes him crave the activity providing a reward but also makes him less likely to pay attention if there is no reward. Medications like Ritalin, which is often prescribed for ADD symptoms, work because they supplement the dopamine activity in the brain, and children who are addicted to video games are, in a sense, medicating themselves by using the games to supplement the dopamine stores in the brain.

Reading

The decrease in attention spans of children today is reflected in how learning and technology is presented to, and consumed by, the young. Parents often remark on how their children get frustrated over a 'slow Internet' when something takes more than a second to load. Consumers of technology, both young and old, demand and expect lightning speed for the delivery of content. A marketing study on converting online visitors to consumers, for example, found that a one-second delay in loading a webpage can result in an over 10 per cent drop in page views; 7 per cent less people are likely to buy from a page that takes one second more time than average in loading, and the customers are likely to be 16 per cent less satisfied.[9]

The link between attention spans and reading may not be obvious at first glance because studies have found that people are actually spending *more* time reading compared to pre-Internet days. What and how they are reading, however, is vastly different.

Reading material on the web consists mostly of blog posts, articles, news and social media posts. These are much more likely to be read if they are already in bulleted form.[10] It seems that consumers demand and expect the information presented to them in an easily digestible form, with the key points clearly spelt out and defined. When information is presented in this manner, it does sift out the chaff from the grain and encourages the writer to be clear and succinct. What is lost, for writer and reader alike, is the deepening of argument and reflective nuances of thought. It also makes it less likely that the reader's brain will do the work to think deeply and to formulate thoughts.

The kind of attention required for reading a book is different from that required for surfing the web. Reading a book, an activity that previous generations of children have spent much time on, requires sustained attention and offers few distractions. It also nurtures imagination and memory. Nicholas Carr in his seminal book *The Shallows*[11] posits the question: 'Is Google making us stupid?' He explains the different ways that technology engages the readers' attention through the use of a metaphor comparing scuba diving versus jet skiing. In scuba diving, for example, the diver goes deep into a slow-paced environment and takes time to notice the nuances in his environment. A jet-skier, on the other hand, moves swiftly and covers a great distance in a short amount of time. However, he skims the surface of the water and he cannot see beyond it as his surroundings whizz by, giving him no time to notice details or reflect. A study from University College London (UCL) in the

United Kingdom has confirmed that people are performing this 'skimming activity' and that they 'power browse' through various websites and links, rarely returning to the same page again.[12] This kind of skimming engages a different part of the brain than traditional reading. The part of the brain that interprets text and creates meaning is largely inactivated when we do this 'power browsing', because we skim through vast bits of information without processing or contemplation.

Reading on Facebook and Twitter is also this jet-skiing kind of reading. What gets noticed and 'liked' on social media is shorter content. Facebook statuses that are longer than seventy words are less likely to get read or commented on, and Instagram, Snapchat and Pinterest all present information mostly in pictures, bypassing the need to read at all.[13] Memes and Infographics also spread information through the use of pictures rather than words and are extremely popular ways to get a message across. While useful for skimming information, this kind of reading is not intellectually or spiritually satisfying.

When children read educational material on the web, it is full of video-based content and hyperlinked to other information. This can be very beneficial for visual learners, but it can also tempt random web surfing (a term coined to capture skipping from one piece of writing to another) and distraction. Studies show that web surfing and reading articles on the web do not contribute much to retention of information or deepening knowledge. In fact, reading only a text version of an article, without the presence of hyperlinks, is more engaging and entertaining for readers, who are likely to retain more.[14]

It is important to recognize that while children are on the net, they cannot avoid the presence of hyperlinks and advertisements. After all, the mostly free content of the worldwide web sustains itself financially by selling ads and it is in its best interest that people are encouraged to go through stuff quickly, to skim and to visit and click on as many sites as possible. The faster we and our children do this, the more efficiently Google can make a customer profile of us, collect information and use it to sell ads and products.

As long as our children continue to read books as well as blogs and posts, they will have the ability to contemplate and reflect on what they have read, to make associations and conclusions and to nurture their imaginations. This is more than simply an intellectual pursuit. In the age of information democracy, where scholars and students have access to the same information, it will take more than just knowing facts for our children to get ahead in careers and in life. As Ellen Galinsky suggests in her book, *Mind in the Making*, the children who will go on to succeed and lead others will be those who can put facts together in new, innovative and creative ways and derive meaning from text.[15]

Learning and technology

Although there is some evidence that certain kinds of technology can enhance learning, especially for learning-disabled children,[16] parents and educators need to be careful before rushing into 'tech-friendly' learning environments. Some research suggests that technology does not always further learning.

Parents are often pressurized into buying electronic games and videos that promise to make their child into 'Baby Einstein'. There is scant evidence that video games or DVDs enhance learning for young children; in fact, there is evidence that it may actually delay language development and other social skills.[17]

Similarly, research indicates that older children who have Internet access during lectures show a decrease in test performance and the ability to recall the lecture.[18] For example, a school in an economically disadvantaged area in the USA found it disheartening that giving laptops to students actually decreased performance rather than enhanced it, as they had expected.[19] Schools that rush to use technology should pay heed to such studies, and parents need to demand that schools do a more thorough job in evaluating the educational needs of students with a careful cost-benefit analysis before rushing headlong into becoming tech-friendly.

Multitasking

Many children today appear to be master multitaskers. A case in point is Sameer. His mother describes his habits as he gets home from school. He puts his bag down, switches on his desktop (he doesn't have a smartphone yet), and opens these windows: Skype in case his cousin who recently moved to Malaysia is online, Instagram to see what classmates have posted, his school homework website, Google to check up on facts for homework, and Libsyn to listen to the latest episode of Serial, the blockbuster podcast. These are just the basics, to be added to as and when needed. He is a high achiever, say his parents, and manages good grades, so they are pretty lax with him, Internet-wise. 'As long as he gets the grades, we cannot really complain,' says Mom, a proud multi-tasker herself.

One or two parents nod their heads in agreement, while others complain that their children's grades could be better if they focused more attention on homework. It is hard, however, they say, because some teachers demand that children do their homework on the computer. In fact, some posh schools even demand that children get their own iPads to download school books on.

Like other matters, the experts are not unified on whether or not multitasking is good for children. Many do argue that the

Internet and the inherent multitasking do help children to adapt and improve their ability to switch between tasks.

Respected neuroscientists disagree. They stand strongly for the view that multitasking itself is a myth.[20] What appears to be multitasking is actually fast-paced switching from task to task and what is known as 'toggling' of attention—when the attention hovers over several bits and pieces. They maintain that it actually lowers the quality of work produced, and even if the resulting lower quality is not apparent, at the very least, it causes stress to the brain.

Again, the nature of the beast is that it encourages multitasking. A study by Stanford professor and communications expert Clifford Nass, with others,[21] in 2009, found that when children have smartphones, they tend to operate many different media platforms at the same time; in other words, they multitask. The same study also found pre-teens who engage in multitasking behaviour report being more stressed than those who do not.

According to psychology professor David E. Meyer, multitasking leads to a 'mental brownout', in that the brain performs at a suboptimal level because its processing power is compromised.[22]

In another study, Adam Gorlick also found that youngsters who are continuously wired and appear to be multitasking are easily distracted and access irrelevant information. They fared worse on tests designed to test their ability to focus and to efficiently switch between tasks.[23]

Time management and productivity

There is another aspect of multitasking that should be pointed out. The way our children use technology is in small bits throughout the day, often while doing other things. Since they are continuously connected and multitasking, it is difficult to distinguish between their online versus offline time, between work and play.

In a 2010 widely circulated *New York Times* article, Matt Ritchel reports that a girl admitted to sending 27,000 text messages per month, or about 900 a day.[24] Even if it takes only thirty seconds per message, that is over seven hours of her time. Most of that time is unaccounted for because it is hidden among other tasks like homework. Although the same distractions affect adults too, this is particularly alarming for young people because they get habituated to the quick answer. As we know, if the neural groundwork for sustained attention and focus is not laid in childhood, it will be that much more difficult to make it up in the future.

There is another way in which technological distractions affect productivity. In his 1992 book *Flow: The Psychology of Happiness*, Mihály Csíkszentmihályi described flow as a state where the mind is deeply focused and immersed in what it is doing.[25] He explained that this is a state of high productivity and creativity where you can produce your best work. The state of flow, however, is extremely fragile and is easily broken by the pinging of incoming messages, for example. It is for this reason that many people, such as authors or artists, who count on the state of flow to do their best work, rely on apps and websites that block social media when they are working. The draw of the ring or the ping is hard for even adults with already developed neural pathways of self-control to resist. Therefore, for children who have not developed their self-control muscles, it is pretty much impossible. This is important for parents to recognize when they complain that their children are addicted to their phones.

Many people who keep a time log of their daily activities are shocked at how much time is spent on social media and other technology. Technology-related distraction has become such a major issue that it has given birth to a new field called Interruption Science, which studies the impact of distractions on job performance. Researchers at Microsoft, Shamsi and Horvitz have studied how long it takes for people to get back on tasks after such a distraction. According to their research, it takes a significant amount of time because people have to find where they left off; they need to regroup their minds and resettle into the task.[26] Other research by Gloria Mark, with others, has also suggested that such distractions affect our work pace and flow.[27]

Disappearing downtime

Downtime to the brain is what sleep is to the body. It nourishes and reboots. When the brain is hyper-stimulated and connected 24/7, there is no opportunity to avail of this regrowth. The brain needs downtime to process and integrate what it has learnt and experienced. This is usually not a conscious process and happens when we are engaged in another activity altogether. Those who produce art, the written or spoken word, will attest to the idea that the best flashes of insight in the creative process come when one is relaxed and not stimulated.

There is emerging research on how being always connected is impacting children's intelligence.[28] Experts say that our intelligence depends, in part, on how well we can transfer information from working memory to long-term memory. This is an essential step before that information can be used to formulate additional thoughts and used conceptually. Working memory has a smaller capacity than long-term memory simply because its job is to hold the information before we can figure out what to do with it. When too much information is crammed into short-term memory, which is often the case today, that information cannot be processed and is lost.

A lot of information is processed, integrated and downloaded while we are resting or asleep. This de-plugging is essential to its processing. When children are continuously plugged in and on the alert, the brain's ability to download and integrate information is compromised.

It is vital that parents and educators pay heed to attention issues related to technology, because the ability to focus and direct attention is one of the foundations of success for other academic and career pursuits. Hundreds of studies have shown that school success is predicted by three skills that children possess when they enter school—reading, maths, and the ability to focus and pay attention.

Accessing the hold of technology on our children: Reflection questions for parents

❐ Does my child find it hard to unplug from his devices?

❐ Does he appear to be mesmerized by his devices, finding it hard to turn his attention away from them?

❐ Does my child beg and nag to be allowed to play on a digital device even when there are other options available to him?

❐ Can my child pay age-appropriate attention to a single task?

❐ Is my child reading real books every day?

Chapter 4

Impact on Health and Physical Development

I really believe the only way to stay healthy is to eat properly, get your rest and exercise. If you don't exercise and do the other two, I still don't think it's going to help you that much.
—Mike Ditka

Manish, a middle-aged dad of three boys, shared a nostalgic story with me. 'We used to live in a middle class neighbourhood which was alive with boys playing cricket in the street, sometimes late into the night with the help of streetlights. The girls would come out to watch or join us. The whole area was bustling with a festive air as the snack sellers set up their wares to entice the neighbourhood children to buy a snack or ice candy. There was a sense of community and friendship. Even though each household had a single TV set, it would only come on at night for a few hours when the family would gather around it after dinner. The programming was never a pull away from our game of cricket. We never thought of cricket as exercise. It was fun and an integral part of our day. We were physically tired when we went home and so were able to eat heartily and sleep well as a result.

'I recently went back to that neighbourhood to visit an old friend's father who was sick,' he continued. 'It was strangely eerie and quiet. There was no one out on the street, no children, no ice candy man and no snack sellers. When I went into my friend's house, there were several children inside, either on their laptops or smartphones. When I asked what happened to the night cricket, one of the fondest memories of my childhood, I was told that even if a boy or two want to play, they can rarely get a whole team because other boys are indoors on their gadgets. This sends even the cricket diehards back into the house because there is no one to play with. I felt a great sense of loss and sadness that these children would never know the simple pleasure of having access to neighbourhood friends because they are too busy connecting to people far away.'

Although Manish shared his story as one of lost friendship, it evokes how the nature of play and movement has changed for the Net Generation. Play and movement came naturally to children and, until very recently, was an intrinsic part of their schedule once they had finished homework and chores. Sadly, this is becoming one more casualty of the Internet age.

Exercise and movement

In North America, the obesity rates for teens have tripled in the last two decades.[1] While it may make sense that developed nations would struggle with obesity, it is worrying that the USA is followed by China and India as the next two countries dealing with high rates of obesity. The Global Burden of Disease Study 2013 found that China was second only to the USA and the worldwide incidence of obesity in children is worryingly high. Almost a quarter of children in developed countries, over 12 per cent, have a body mass index (BMI) of more than 25 kg/m^2 or greater, which has resulted in an increase in various health issues.[2] While studies show that the amount of TV that children watch has not increased much during this time, the overall screen time certainly has due to other devices—by some estimates, many teenagers spend seven hours or more in front of screens today.[3] Dr Pradeep Chowbey, director of the Institute of Minimal Access and Bariatric Surgery at Max Healthcare

Institute, said in an interview to *India Today*, 'If we see the graph of obesity from 1999 onwards, Indians started gaining weight due to urbanization. There has been gradual economical improvement in our status. The entrance of modern technology and Internet has turned people lazy and stagnant.'[4]

So, while digital technology by itself is not entirely to blame for this phenomena, the fact that 'teens manipulate a joystick instead of a baseball bat'[5] to engage in play does not help their need for movement. For many children, like the ones in Manish's neighbourhood, screen time has replaced outdoor play as the leisure activity of choice.

Exercise has many more benefits than just keeping children's weight in check. Research has found a long list of benefits from exercise which are particularly valuable for children today, such as reducing stress, increasing energy and productivity, improving mood, alleviating symptoms of depression and anxiety, sharpening memory and improving sleep, to name a few.[6]

Many parents I have spoken to are unaware of how common depression and anxiety are among children, especially teens. The incidence and diagnoses of depression and anxiety has gone up several hundred per cent in the last couple of decades, according to Professor Mark Reinecke, Chief, Division of Psychology at Northwestern University. He says that in any given educational institution in North America, about 5 per cent of teens are depressed at any one time.[7] In an age where there has been a significant increase in mental health issues for children and adolescents, notably depression and anxiety, it seems that exercise is an easy and inexpensive way to improve mental and physical well-being with almost no downsides. It makes sense that parents should endeavour to encourage the habit of play, movement and exercise in young children so that it becomes an integral part of their daily lives.

On the technology front, it is not all bad news. The purveyors of gaming technology have begun to respond. With the emergence of 'exergaming' devices, such as Wii and Xbox Kinect, gaming has begun to incorporate physical activity. Some of the most popular games, such as Wii Sports, allow children to play virtual games such as tennis and baseball. According to a study presented to the American College of Sports Medicine, participating in exergaming requires at least twice the amount of energy as traditional video gaming, and can raise children's activity levels to a moderate-intensity one.[8] Additionally, it provides an opportunity for family and friends to play together and is a social activity for users. However, it is not advisable to replace all activity with Wii gaming as it lacks the sensory experience of the real game and an opportunity to be outdoors and connect with nature, which is also essential for mental and physical well-being.

There are other murmurs about the direct impact of technology on physical health. In a disturbing study from the UK, it was reported that more than two-thirds of primary schoolchildren had reported experiencing neck and back pain from March–September 2011. Helena Webb, paediatric physiotherapist at the ABM University Health Board in West Glamorgan, said that children are facing a 'time bomb' of musculoskeletal health issues directly related to the use of computers and smartphones. Webb mentioned that the number of children receiving treatment for back and neck pain in her practice had doubled over a six-month period, and even more disturbing was that among the 204 children (aged seven to eighteen) who were part of the study, 90 per cent said that they had not mentioned the pain to anyone.[9] Webb went on to caution that short periods of exercise may not be enough to counteract the impact of sitting for long periods of time, and that it was recommended that children change their position and walk around several times an hour to maintain musculoskeletal health.

Wi-Fi radiation and cancer risk

A quick search on the Internet will reveal many alternative health websites cautioning about cell phone use and increased cancer risk—these voices are not yet in the mainstream. As of now, the American Cancer Society says there is no evidence of increased risk of brain tumours or other types of cancers associated with cell phone radiation. However, the International Agency for Research on Cancer (IARC), part of the United Nations' World Health Organization (WHO), classifies radio frequency electromagnetic fields (RF/EMF) as Class 2B Carcinogens, possibly carcinogenic to humans.[10] The main sources of RF/EMF are radios, televisions, microwave ovens, cell phones and Wi-Fi devices. Health authorities in Europe and other parts of the world, such as Russia, are taking heed.

Dr Lennart Hardell from the University Hospital in Orebro, Sweden, the lead researcher of a widely publicized study in 2008, advised that mobile phone use before the age of twenty was particularly problematic and correlated with a more than five-fold increase in glioma, a cancer of the glial cells that support the central nervous system.[11] 'The risk is three times higher after twenty-five years of use. We can see this clearly,' oncologist Dr Lennart Hardell told Reuters.[12]

In a 2011 resolution, the Council of Europe declared, '…there could be extremely high human and economic costs if early warnings are neglected.' It recommended that the As Low As Reasonably Achievable (ALARA) principle be applied to electromagnetic radiation emissions. Following this warning, some European countries, such as France, are pressing for bills to limit or ban Wi-Fi in maternity wards and childcare facilities, and provide for consultations from parent groups before installing Wi-Fi routers in schools.[13]

In Switzerland, strict new regulations around Wi-Fi installation in schools are accompanied by an aggressive public awareness campaign about the health risks of RF radiation. Fewer than a hundred of Switzerland's 6,800 schools have wireless connections, opting instead for wired connections because they are deemed to be safer and 'because there's no reason to put a radiation source that isn't absolutely necessary in schools'. Russian school authorities also limit radiation exposure in schools. Oleg Grigoriev, chairman of the Russian National Committee on Non-Ionizing Radiation Protection (an expert group that reports to the Russian parliament), maintains that Russian researchers have shown links with damage to children's cognitive function caused by long-term exposure to low-strength electromagnetic fields.[14]

In the developing world, by contrast, there is much less public discourse about the possible harmful effects from Wi-Fi radiation. Although public health authorities across the globe may not be unified in acknowledging the risks, as parents we cannot wait while scientists battle it out. As Devra Davis, PhD, MPH, president of the Environmental Health Trust, points out, we know that exposure to this 'unnatural bath of radiation' damages DNA and impairs natural cellular repair processes, a phenomenon that may lead to cancer.[15] Yet, we are proceeding with this large-scale, uncontrolled experiment anyway.

Since children are still developing, they have rapid cellular replication and growth rates that make them especially vulnerable to DNA damage. They also have a longer lifetime exposure to this new pervasive radiation than any previous generation.

It is, therefore, important for parents to educate themselves about the possible risks and make informed choices about using

Wi-Fi technology, such as not leaving it on continuously even when not used.

Developmental milestones

Developmental milestones are behaviours or physical skills seen in babies and children as they grow, such as crawling, walking and talking, and they are one way for parents and doctors to confirm that a child is healthy and developing well. These milestones must not be taken as an exact schedule for the child but rather as broad guidelines of developmental tasks that children need to accomplish at certain age ranges. Child development experts believe that achieving milestones for the vast majority of children is not complicated. As long as they are given opportunities to move, to play and to connect with people, in addition to being provided the basic physical needs, children will do well. As they grow and become adolescents and young adults, their healthy development consists of acquiring life skills, such as cooking and driving, which will allow them to live an independent, responsible life.

According to a growing number of medical experts and other health professionals, the active or passive technology use by young children can potentially affect their physical, mental, social and emotional development significantly. In an age where tablets and smartphones are an integral part of children's lives, there is emerging research that our tech-savvy children are growing to adolescence without basic life skills. In other words, the inappropriate and excessive use of technology has the potential to interrupt both healthy development in children and adolescents. In 2009, the British Columbia's Society of Occupational Therapists reported, 'Children now rely on technology for the majority of their play, grossly limiting necessary challenges to their bodies in order to achieve optimal sensory and motor development...with subsequent impact on achieving basic foundation skills necessary for literacy.'[16] A more recent study in 2014 has confirmed that children are entering school without basic life skills due to digital device overuse. The study reported that more than half of children aged between two and ten can confidently use a tablet but do not know how to swim, tell the time or tie their own shoelaces.[17] In the UK, research has found similar results. In a survey of 2,000 parents of children aged two to sixteen years, research found that about 30 per cent of children aged two to four owned or had access to tablet computers. Parents of these children reported that they were concerned about device overuse and also reported that their children are more likely to learn to use a mobile phone before being able to ride a bike or learn to read.[18]

Teachers are often the first adults outside the family who have frequent access to our children. Moreover, experienced teachers have the benefit of having interacted with different cohorts of children in different age groups. Such teachers and educators have been sounding the alarm that children today are very tech savvy but often lacking in basic life skills. I met with a group of teachers after a workshop to discuss their experiences with children exposed to technology. Geeta, a public school teacher who has spent over thirty years teaching young children from two and a half to six year ages said, 'I find many toddlers today are extremely comfortable using a smartphone or tablet. While I have counselled my school's parents not to allow young children to play with their devices, clearly they are not heeding the message. My children at school these days are very adept at swiping and clicking, showing that they are familiar with mobile technology. What I find, however, is that their fine motor skills in activities such as cutting with scissors, writing with a pencil, or even tying their shoelaces are less developed than they have been in previous generations.' Many teachers present nodded in agreement, indicating that this is not an uncommon experience.

Sleep and rest

Sleep is just as important as diet and exercise for health and well-being. The way people function when they are awake depends, at least in part, on how well they sleep. While we are sleeping, the body is working to support healthy brain function and to maintain physical health. Sleep is particularly important for children and adolescents because it supports brain development and physical growth. Parents and experts are united in their concern that technology is greatly compromising the quality of our children's sleep.

The average twelve-year-old goes to sleep around 9 p.m. and sleeps for about nine hours, whereas experts believe that ten to eleven hours per night is the ideal sleep time for seven- to twelve-year-olds. Teens need between ten to eleven hours of sleep, but many of them do not get nearly enough sleep, leading to constant crabbiness and irritability brought on by chronic sleep deprivation.

Firstly, many children take their devices to bed, hiding under the covers and texting or playing games. The light and energy from the digital devices interrupts and decreases melatonin production, an essential hormone for sleep. When melatonin production is disrupted, it gives a signal to the body that it is time to wake up. The lights from digital technology can also cause the temperature of the body to rise slightly, which also messes up the sleep cycle as it is normal for the body temperature to drop at night when the body naturally prepares itself for sleep.[19]

Secondly, playing games hyper-stimulates the mind instead of winding it down. The Kaiser Family Foundation found that when children consume digital media content before bedtime, it increases stress and arousal hormones in the body, making it harder for them to go to sleep and get a good-quality rest.[20]

Thirdly, given that time is a scarce commodity, the more digital media children consume, the less physical activity they will engage in. The *Archives of Disease in Childhood* reports that the less physical activity children engage in, the harder it is for them to fall asleep. And physically active children fall asleep quicker, sleep deeply and tend to stay asleep for longer.[21]

Additionally, if children take their devices to bed and text or instant message friends at night, they are in the midst of a cycle of conversation, which keeps them awake. Research has found that children between the ages of eleven and thirteen sleep significantly less when they use technology for recreation or study before bedtime. Even studying on a computer was found to impact children who reported using SNSs before bedtime and then slept a full hour less than their unplugged peers. This is quite disturbing as the length and quality of sleep in children has been linked to many medical issues such as depression, mood swings, lower grades, as well as obesity. A study from Dalhousie University in Canada found that even slight sleep deprivation has a great impact on children's academic and social functioning.[22]

Summary of action points for parents

- ❏ Encourage daily physical activity and free play.
- ❏ Ensure that your children learn basic life skills of daily living in addition to being good at using technology.
- ❏ Keep cell phones and other technological devices out of bedrooms where children sleep.
- ❏ Have a technology curfew from an hour before bedtime to thirty minutes after rising.

Chapter 5

Faking It on Facebook: Impact on Self-image

People who have so much of their personality invested in the Internet can't really survive as whole individuals without it.
—Mark A. Rayner

Presentation anxiety

Expert psychologists are increasingly focusing on how digital media is shaping the identities and personalities of adolescents. The Internet, especially social media, has the potential to impact the self-image and emotional health of children, particularly adolescents. 'There is a lot of pressure for my generation to get our social media profiles just right. It is, you know, going to be seen and judged by many people. If we get it right, it can raise our "sick (that is, cool) potential". Get it wrong and it is, like, you know, social suicide,' says Sana, a bright, attractive sixteen-year-old who attends therapy sessions for depression and anxiety.

Academics come easily to Sana, who does well in school and hopes to study medicine in the future. Although she finds school easy, Sana does not enjoy it and finds it hard to make friends. She says she is 'very active' on social media but that she has a complicated relationship with Facebook. Describing herself as 'socially awkward', she said that when she first discovered Facebook, she was excited because she thought it would be easier to make friends as her social awkwardness would not be obvious. She started sending friend requests to many of the cool children in her school who were 'out of her social league'. She soon found that the online world of friendship was no easier. 'I feel that there are rules about social networking sites which are made by the cool people, but which losers like me try to follow so that we can join the cool crowd.'

Sana confesses that she has always been an anxious child but that Facebook has given her an entirely new level of anxiety. She agonizes over her online profile, deciding which 'dp' (display picture) to use, editing and re-editing her wall so that it will get a maximum number of 'likes'. She posts pictures and 'selfies' strategically, after looking at what cool people post. She keeps track of how many 'likes' her pictures get, compared to the number of 'likes' that posts by her popular cousin attract. The comments that her friends make about her pictures greatly impact her, but if somebody else posts her picture, she asks them to delete it because 'I am not photogenic and don't want people to judge me based on those pictures.'

Her popular cousin Nabila, who is in the same class as her, has a very different relationship with social media. Nabila, an easy-going and self-assured young lady, posts about her interests, different social causes and the various interest groups she is a part of, from jazz to spiritual feminism to knitting. Both are active on social media and have vibrant Facebook profiles, but their differing relationship with social media reveals a great deal about their sense of self.

If they are away from Facebook, both girls miss it. Nabila says that she misses out on what her friends are up to and enjoys catching up at least once a day on what is going on in the virtual world. She also checks on the various interest groups to see if there are articles or events of interest. In between checking Facebook, Instagram and Twitter, she keeps in touch with friends via instant messaging and Skype. Sana, on the other hand, does not have that many friends to instant message and her time on social media consists mostly of 'stalking' people and their friends. She accepts anyone who wants to be her friend on Facebook or other platforms and sends friend requests even after meeting a person casually only once. Sana spends much longer on Facebook and feels down when she is signing off. She reports being envious of her Facebook friends' lives.

Psychologists explain that the reason why SNSs like MySpace and Facebook are so popular is that they satisfy a basic human need, the need to be seen, to be known, to connect with others, and for others to like us. Human beings are hardwired to connect and, in a sense, we find and define ourselves in relationship with others of our species.[1]

When children are young, their social circle revolves around parents and families. As they become adolescents, peers become increasingly important. One of the key tasks of adolescent development is to form self-identity and a healthy self-image, to be okay with who they are and what they look like.[2] It is a time when children are trying to forge their own identity, trying to become independent of parents, but getting closer to peers because they play a large role in forming an adolescent's identity and image.[3] The opinions of peers on everything, from clothes to hairstyle to what is cool, begin to matter more.

Many of us who were children and adolescents in the pre-digital age will remember gathering friends' comments and opinions about us in 'slam books'. At the end of the year, we would also encourage our friends to write in the annual school yearbook. We would then go home, find a quiet place and pore over the comments they made, looking for validation that we were loved, that we mattered, that we belonged and were accepted in our group of friends.

Narcissism

With the advent of the digital age and the continuous connectivity to peers, approval-seeking from peers, a normal part of adolescent behaviour, is much more intense. Social media allows young people to craft a persona that they want the world to see. It allows children to put their 'best face forward,' says Jeffrey Hancock, associate professor of communication at Cornell University, and present a personality that is likely to get the maximum positive attention from peers.[4] While it is normal to have an idealized self, a self that one aspires to be, Facebook profiles are not that, he explains. The profiles are not based on the ideal of our best self—they are crafted and based almost entirely on what the peer group expects and will respond to. In a real-life peer group, teens are able to read body language and non-verbal signs about what is and is not acceptable. In the world of Facebook, however, where the vast majority of messages are positive ones, it is silence or lack of comments which is the only potentially negative feedback. The silence needs interpreting, as one is never sure why there are no comments or no feedback from friends. 'Is the post lame, unacceptable or loser-ish, or is it simply that my friends are busy and didn't get around to commenting? It is torture never to know the answer to this,' remarked Sana. Professor Hancock believes that the climate of social media, which thrives on giving friends feedback through 'likes', tends to skew the developing sense of self.[5]

Psychologists are currently studying 'presentation anxiety', which is very common among young adolescents active on social media.[6] Theodera Stites wrote a poignant essay about presentation anxiety and the psychology of social media in the *New York Times* saying, 'Every profile is a carefully planned media campaign. I click on the Friendster "Who's Viewed Me" tab to see who has stumbled upon my profile recently, and if people I don't know have checked me out, I immediately check them back. I get an adrenaline rush when I find out that a friend of a friend I was always interested in is evidently interested in me, too.'[7]

Recently, researchers have started looking at the relationship between self-esteem and 'presentation anxiety' on social media. Although there is no clear consensus whether Facebook causes low self-esteem or whether it is people with low esteem who engage in heavy Facebook use, there are some clear trends.[8]

Research by S.S. Sundar and his colleagues found that the way people use social media, such as Facebook, reveals their underlying self-concept and sense of self.[9] In the earlier days of social media, psychologists had expected that since sharing parts of our lives with friends is important for bonding, it would improve friendships. In fact, research from Cornell University suggests that Facebook can also boost confidence and self-esteem in young adults when peers encourage and cheer them on by commenting on their Facebook statuses.[10] A study published in *Psychological Science* found, however, that people with high self-confidence and self-esteem benefit from SNSs.[11] People with low self-esteem, or those who have trouble with friendships in real life, tend to share more negative aspects of their lives and this makes them less attractive to their peers.

Sundar also found that people who have low self-worth usually monitor their profiles more and are more concerned about comments and posts from their peers. They are more likely to post personal information which is designed to draw favourable attention via sympathy and kindness, but often has the opposite effect and tends to turn people away.[12]

Young people like Nabila, who are generally comfortable in their own skins and have high self-esteem, are more likely to post information about family, about their interests and pursuits, about education and work. They use Facebook mainly to 'self-publish' or share aspects from their lives and work and tend to be less concerned with what and how many comments they get on each post. Other studies have also shown that what children post on their profiles reveals their level of insecurity or low self-esteem. Researchers at York University found that young adults who engaged in 'self-promotion' on Facebook, frequently updating their statuses, posting glamorous pictures of themselves and boasting about their accomplishments, tended to be more insecure and narcissistic than those who did not.[13]

So it appears that narcissistic tendencies are related to SNSs but not in the way we might think. Those that appear most narcissistic and self-absorbed are trying to use social media to boost their self-image rather than to show off an already confident and healthy sense of self.

Research has also found that all things being equal, if you are on Facebook, it is better to be an active user, posting content rather than passively viewing other people's content. A study by Burke et al. found that passive consumption of Facebook information, also known as 'stalking', was correlated with feelings of loneliness.[14] In other words, when children browse other people's profiles without sharing parts of their lives, they are more likely to be lonely and use social media to alleviate negative emotions.

Selfies and body image

Adolescence is a time of major hormonal and physical changes that cause many to become preoccupied with their appearance. Before the age of social media, adolescents fretting over whether they were good-looking or clever enough used to be a private affair—between the adolescent and the mirror and, maybe, shared with a close friend or a diary. With the advent of social media, specifically Facebook, Instagram and, more recently, the posting of 'selfies', the arena of body image angst has moved to the public stage. Where previously teens could look in the mirror and wonder if they were good-looking enough, now they post pictures of themselves on social media sites which, subject to comments by their peers, greatly increase anxiety about body image.

Secondly, before social media, teens used to look at fashion magazines, drool over supermodels and compare their own bodies to them. While doing that comes with its own set of issues, it was clear that not every teen could look fabulous (although many tried). When teens compare themselves to those they see as social equals, their group of friends, it appears to bring a deeper level of angst.

To add to the complications, there are unknown adults present in virtual space. Unlike a conversation in real time where one has a sense of who is around and may overhear a particular communication, teens often forget that in the audience are adults who do not understand the social references. So, while they choose to give a particular impression to a section of their peer group ('strutting'), they do not realize that there are many others who will take this out of context. They also choose their own terms to identify themselves; for example, in 'with lots of siblings', 'married' to a friend and so on, which are inside jokes and references that only a peer group would get. Much of this can be considered harmless fun and peer groups often 'get it'—they may not hold the young person to a particular exposure of identity which could or could not be part of who they eventually choose to be.

A particularly sad story was told by Lubna, an observant young Muslim girl. She comes from a strict family and generally follows the rules laid down by her parents. She said she used an alias as a Facebook name, because she did not want to be searchable by her parents, or worse, her parent's friends, who would be very judgemental about her friends. After some persuasion, she was able to get permission to spend the night at a friend's house. The friends were fooling around, pretending to raid the father's bar and drink. The girls held glasses in their hands and posed, taking pictures and laughing. The girls were long-time friends, understood each other's situations and were careful not to post any pictures on social media. The trouble was that no one really paid much attention to her friend's young cousin who was playing around with her phone and taking pictures, which later showed up on Facebook. To make matters worse, her mother came across the pictures through another profile and had, what Lubna called 'a hissy fit'. Sadly, the mother did not understand that being photographed with a beer did not mean that the girls were drinking. Sadly also, for Lubna, although the young cousin was persuaded to take the pictures down, neither Lubna or her friends can be sure of how many people had seen it and what kind of digital footprint it has left. Lubna's mother, after a conversation with Lubna, is now reassured that her daughter was not drinking, but is rather worried that others will see that picture and judge her.

So although many children think that they are fully in control of what they share, they may lose sight of the fact that others may share their pictures and comments, which may end up where they were never meant to be. The quest for identity is made complicated by the fact that self-publications may be taken out of context and the digital footprints left behind may concretize their personality for others, while they themselves have outgrown that particular stage. In the old days, such moments, captured only in baby pictures, were seen by very few people!

As Sherry Turkle says in *Alone Together*, forming an identity is stressful for young people today '…presenting a self in these circumstances, with multiple media and multiple goals, is not easy work.'[15]. 'It is hard enough to figure out who you are without every adult making a judgement of you without any idea of the context,' says one young person.

Facebook envy

The feeling of envy is generated when we want something that someone else has. Envy takes root because we feel inferior in stature or possessions to someone else. People generally judge their own success and happiness in comparison to others. Social media networks such as MySpace and Facebook provide an easy and tempting platform in which to engage in social comparisons with peers.[16] Facebook friends groups are generally made up of people with similar backgrounds and social standing, making social comparisons all the more painful.

Comparing ourselves to our peers instead of celebrities is much more painful, because we understand that famous people 'are out of our league' and because we don't know them personally. Experts believe that why Facebook-users, including adolescents, are falling prey to Facebook-generated envy is because they compare ourselves to a manicured image of someone whom they know, who is part of their social circle, at least online.[17] When we see a person in real life, we are more likely to get a complete picture of them, 'warts and all'. In social media profiles, we get to see only the best parts of their life, carefully edited to generate admiration and attention, if not envy. According to research, it is the social interactions and perceived happiness of others which causes the most envy.

To manage envy, children may try greater self-promotion and 'impression management', crafting their online persona to an extent that barely resembles them. Once again, children and young adults who have issues with self-esteem are the most vulnerable to these feelings.

Facebook statuses give rise to envy because the profile that people craft online focuses on the positive. They post the best pictures of their vacations, their birthday celebrations and their academic and career successes. In the Stanford University study conducted by Alex Jordan, Jordan found that Facebook-users consistently overestimated the good times and positive experiences that their friends had, further impacting emotional and psychological well-being.[18] When we see pictures of others on Facebook, we look at a posed and framed image—for example, we do not see the fights the family had before, or that two brothers smiling in the picture are not on talking terms with each other. In real-life interactions, you get a fuller picture of the other. Additionally, people who lack the financial or social means to engage in what others are doing experience dissatisfaction. As a young lady from a wealthy background shared in my office tearfully, she had posted pictures of the cruise her family took for her sixteenth birthday, as that is what she thought everyone was expected to do. 'But a couple of my friends posted nasty comments on my wall, saying how I was showing off.'

Body image

We live in an age of extreme consciousness about physical appearances. Girls are becoming conscious at younger ages, and the media plays a huge role in establishing what the desirable physical attributes are, especially for women, but also for young men. Recently, I have noticed many young men come into my clinic with body image related issues.

A study conducted by the Eating Disorders Centre at Sheppard Pratt Hospital found that a significant proportion of young Facebook-users spend a lot of time comparing their bodies to others on Facebook through posted pictures and profiles. Dr Harry Brandt commented that in the age of digital technology, it was very difficult for young people to avoid triggers that cause a negative body image.[19] Unlike pictures in magazines, Facebook profiles tend to be people we know, making the comparisons all the more glaring.

Another study, published in the *International Journal of Eating Disorders*, found a link between social media use and body image issues, including eating disorders. The study found that young women, in particular, who spent more than twenty minutes at a time on social media, showed signs of 'appearance-focused behaviour' (such as anorexia) and were more anxious about their body image.[20]

Social psychologist Ethan Kross from the University of Michigan believes that rather than enhancing well-being for users, frequent use of Facebook actually undermines it.[21] These findings are confirmed in another study from Manchester's University of Salford, where a full 50 per cent of the 298 participants reported that social networks such as Facebook and Twitter made their lives less happy and that their own sense of self-worth and self-esteem suffers when they compare their own lives and accomplishments to those of their Facebook friends.[22]

So, what parents need to ask is, as Christine Rosen points out in the *Digital Divide*, what kind of behaviour does social networking encourage? At an age when children are trying to forge their own identity, there is pressure to give up privacy, to share intimate and yet emerging details of one's psyche and identity, which may cause others to respond with envy or create anxiety about their own lot in life.[23] While giving up social media may not be a route that most families are willing to take, it is clear that being bored, unhappy and lonely in one's real life makes it very tempting to retreat to the virtual world.

Reality TV

We are living in an age where success is defined as the ability to attract attention, writes David Brooks, the *New York Times* columnist.[24] It is often difficult for the older generation to comprehend what people like Paris Hilton or the Kardashians are famous for—except for the fact that, well, they are famous! The dream of stardom is now available to everyone with an Internet connection. It is the age of broadcast—and we can all have our own TV shows and access to our own TV channels. This is positive in that it is very democratic and levels the playing field. In the wrong hands, however, it generates rubbish. Sixteen-year-old Nina tells the story of someone she knew who started an online presence and, 'just for fun', started to post seductive pictures of herself. Soon, she attracted thousands of 'likes' from middle-aged men. Since she used an alias and was careful not to 'friend' anyone she knew in real life, her game went on for quite some time undetected by parents and other family members. Just an innocent girl, she was lured into being who she thought she should be. Of course, her mother was devastated when she found out.

It can be very difficult for children to judge what is wrong when so many others seem to be doing the same thing and getting a lot of attention for it.

Reflection questions and action points for parents

❏ Have you seen your children's social media profile? Their friends' profiles?

❏ Do they contain any of the issues we talked about in this chapter?

❏ What do the profiles emphasize? Looks, achievements, or possessions?

❏ Discuss your child's profile with her. What message does she want to send? Is that the message that is being received?

❏ Are your children aware of who the potential audience of their posts is?

Chapter 6

The Impact on Relationships and Communication

The single biggest problem in communication is the illusion that it has taken place.
—George Bernard Shaw

The Karim family is fairly typical of today's families. Mom works part-time and is home before the children. By the time Dad comes home, the rest of the family is settled into its own little private world of technology. The twins are playing a video game after homework and the eldest daughter is on Facebook. Mom is catching up on email. When Dad walks in, they barely look up from their devices to say 'Hi'.

Communications and connections

We have long known the importance of strong relationships for emotional well-being and happiness. Research shows that healthy relationships do more than contribute to happiness. They are correlated to longevity, stress management and physical health.[1] It is important, then, that as parents we pay particular attention to the quality of relationships that our children develop, as healthy bonds will set them up for a lifetime of well-being.

Communication is vital to developing relationships. It is through listening and talking together that we get to know each other, build intimacy, express what is important to us, as well as support the other. Communication experts have explained that words, although vital, are only a part of effective communication. Body language, tone of voice and context of communication are all important in building closeness and understanding between individuals.[2]

This chapter will explore the new platforms of communication and how they are impacting our relationships and the ability of our children to form relationships.

Friendship and virtual intimacy

Right now, I am trying to make friends outside of Facebook while applying the same principles. So every day, I walk in the street and tell people what I ate, how I feel, what I did the day before, what I am doing, what I will do next...I also listen to the conversations of others and tell them 'I like!' And it works!

Result: I already have three people who are following me: two policemen and one psychiatrist.
—Facebook Post

Everyone agrees that the Internet has had a major impact on social life and on relationships. While some researchers talk about how this connectivity allows people and groups to connect without geographical or time boundaries, others contend that it is sterile and has a negative impact on communication. While there is no argument about the fact that digital technology has enabled connectivity and communication on an unprecedented scale, there are also increasingly loud murmurs that technology has changed the very nature and definition of communication and relationships for our families.[3]

The quote above is a case in point. The reason I believe this quote is going viral on Facebook is because it captures the nature and quality of online friendships. Social media has blurred the lines between friends, acquaintances and strangers, and possibly redefined what friendship itself means.

Friendship on Facebook generally means that your 'friend'

will engage in personal broadcasting to as wide an audience possible. When others read the posts, they get the illusion that they really know the person. What they know, however, is not the real-life person but a carefully crafted online profile which is based on what the person wishes to share.

The reason it is important to talk about online socializing is because more than 75 per cent of young people use a social media platform to initiate or maintain friendships.[4] Friendships are an integral part of healthy development in children because they encourage important social skills, such as communication, cooperation, tolerance, solving problems, dealing with hurt and rejection, and so on.[5]

Children and adolescents have always wanted to squeeze in as much time with friends as possible, and with online social networking, this has become possible. They can stay in touch all the time, with many friends at the same time; they can increase their social status by displaying the number of friends they have; they can find and make friends with others who share similar interests even though they may live very far away.

If young people are using the Internet to cement friendships that they already have, and if they still have the time and opportunity to continue to relate to others face-to-face, the Internet can be a valuable tool for social connection.

There are, however, some factors about connecting online that parents need to be aware of. Many children, even if private by nature, feel a lot of social pressure to have many friends on social media sites, such as Facebook. Their profiles, rather than containing their true identity, are carefully constructed to be acceptable to their peer group, and many will stress over what to list as favourite movies and books, even if they don't really care about the people on their friends' list. Experts are concerned that while this may give the illusion of friendship, there are some key differences.[6]

In the *New York Times* article, 'How to Be Liked by Everyone Online', Pamela Paul writes that 'to friend' has become a verb, and unlike real-life friendships, Facebook friendships can be started and ended with the click of the keyboard, changing the meaning of the word. Experts are concerned that this quick making and ending of friendships may be redefining the meaning of friendship for young people. On the other hand, SNSs may also be prolonging relationships which we have naturally outgrown. 'Friendships' such as these may add little to social connections other than to inflate one's friends' list and maybe pressure one to wish others on birthdays and so on.[7]

Research from the University of California, Los Angeles (UCLA) lends credibility to the theory that the idea of friendship itself has changed for the Net Generation. Patricia Greenfield, a UCLA developmental psychologist and the director of the Children's Digital Media Center in Los Angeles, has found that young people report feeling socially supported by having large networks of online friends, not necessarily friends they ever see face-to-face.[8] In other words, it has become desirable to gather as many friends as possible, for those with a larger friends' list have more social credibility.

It is interesting that earlier, Oxford anthropologist and evolutionary psychologist Robin Dunbar—who is famous for his 'Dunbar number' regarding the number of friends a person can have cognitively—had discovered that based on the size of an adult brain, the average human can have around 150 people in his or her social group, and that anything more than that is too complex for most of us to process. He found that 150 was the outermost group of social connections one could maintain.[9] This further begs the question of the purpose and goal of an inflated friends list. Dunbar stressed that close friendships are, of course, much fewer.

At the same time, some research suggests that our 'inner circle' of friendships, those whom we are truly intimate with, is shrinking. Cornell University's Professor Brashear conducted a study on friendship where he interviewed 2,000 adults about their close relationships. He found that adults reported that the number of friends that the participants could discuss 'important matters' with had fallen from an average of three in 1985 to just about two.[10] Professor Brashear's survey also found that about a quarter of the population in the USA said that they did not have *anyone* with whom they could talk about important matters. This figure was double of what it was in 1985.[11] This disturbing figure showing that a quarter of the population is lonely would appear to be a natural result of a trend where people gather a large number of friends without paying attention to building relationships with a few people which, of course, takes more time and effort. It appears that some young people prefer to spend time at home and do personal broadcasting with people they hardly know, rather than spend time chatting to a close friend. Personal broadcasting, or sharing with a wide audience, requires a different skill set than face-to-face communication with one person. It seems that the Net Generation is privileging connection over intimacy, and social isolation and loneliness in a world of hyper-connectivity is growing.

There is reason to suggest that the Net Generation has other issues with close relationships. Consider the *New York Times* article by Theodora Stites, which we discussed earlier. Stites writes: 'I'm 24 years old, have a good job, friends. But like many of my generation, I consistently trade actual human contact for the more reliable emotional high of smiles on MySpace, winks on Match.com and pokes on Facebook. I live for Friendster views, profile comments and the Dodgeball messages that clog my cell phone every night.

'I prefer, in short, a world cloaked in virtual intimacy. It may be electronic, but it is intimacy nevertheless. Besides, eye contact isn't all it's cracked up to be and facial expressions can be so hard to control. My life goes like this: Every morning, before I brush my teeth, I sign in to my Instant Messenger to let everyone know I'm awake. I check for new e-mail, messages or views, bulletins, invitations, friend requests, comments on my blog or mentions of me or my blog on my friends' blogs.'[12]

The new rules of communication

The Net Generation's preferred mode of communication is via text or instant messaging. A recent Pew Research Center study found that two-thirds of those surveyed said they were more likely to use their cell phones to text friends than to call them. Only 33 per cent said that they talk to their friends face-to-face on a daily basis.[13] We know the vast majority of communication is non-verbal, through tone of voice and body language. This means that text and instant messaging conversations are stripping away 93 per cent of the context of conversations. Moreover, what remains is not words but abbreviations and emoticons, which can be used to express a wide variety of meanings by the sender and interpreted in as many ways by the receiver.

Many argue that the variety of emoticons and phrases is developing into a vast, rich vocabulary to convey meaning and emotion in a text conversation. However, I would argue that this is far from perfect. There is a rapport in communication, which means that if your words and language is mismatching your non-verbals, I can pick up on the mismatch when I am face-to-face with you. Even if I am talking on the telephone, I can pick up subtle cues in your tone and pitch. So even if you say 'I am fine', I can tell that you are not by, for example, the tone of your voice. This is entirely missing in a text conversation.

Occasionally, it may be helpful to self-censor what you are going to say in a conversation to avoid hurting someone's feelings, for example. On a continuous basis, this is not effective for relationship-building or intimacy because the other cannot 'hear' you fully and thereby build intimacy.

So why is it so increasingly common for youth to use text rather than face-to-face communication? I spoke to many young people in an effort to find out what the attraction to text messages was as opposed to talking to friends. Here are the some of the reasons that came up again and again:

'It is difficult for me to talk about feelings. I feel weak and vulnerable when I do that. It is much easier to hide feelings when we are chatting via text.'

'I can edit and re-edit the message before sending it, controlling what and how much I say.'

'Texting is way more efficient than calling. Why would you want to call when you can text? With texting, you say exactly what you want to and don't have to engage in unnecessary talk. A "YO" is enough small talk.'

'With texting, there is less social awkwardness. You don't have to deal with awkward silences.'

'With texting, you don't have to respond right away. You can think about what you want to say. Although there is great pressure sometimes to reply right away, otherwise your friend might think you are mad at them.'

'If my friend is sad or upset, I would rather read it via text than listen to her cry. Then I don't get so sad.'

'It is easier to say difficult things via text. I admit I have broken up with a girlfriend by sending her a text. I did feel sad about it. But I did not want to deal with her crying and being upset in person. Everyone does it these days. It's kinda expected that if things are not working out, you expect a text to say it's over.'

As you can see, many young people desire to control the

level of intimacy in a relationship by controlling communication. They firmly believe that control over the time and effort spent makes it easier and more efficient.

It may be true that it is certainly easier in the short term to deal with the emotional ups and downs at a distance. When you can see pain (and joy) in someone else's eyes, which may sometimes be caused by you, it is uncomfortable. The problem is that human relationships cannot be founded on efficiency. It also means that avoiding the discomfort of witnessing pain and joy loses the essence of human connection, which comes from witnessing the emotions of another.

While few would disagree that texts are more 'efficient' than making a phone call, they only give the illusion of efficient 'connection' and 'communication' and fall short for many reasons:

1. Although how and when you will communicate is controlled, you rarely get the intended message across because so much communication is lost with the missing tone of voice and body language.

2. It is also true that you do not have to deal with the emotional 'messiness' of human interaction. Young people often remark how the absence of face-to-face contact makes it easier to deal with emotions. What researchers have found, however, is that the lack of supplemental information, such as facial expression and tone of voice, makes children and teens more unsure about the meaning behind the message—they may spend a great deal of time trying to decode the messages and making sense of them, causing themselves a great deal of anxiety. When teens take part in a group chat, which has become increasingly common since the advent of WhatsApp messaging, it is very easy to misunderstand who is saying what to whom.

   Sally shared that in her class friends' group chat, she

notices that one person always ignores her messages and as soon as she has shared something, will 'hijack the conversation' by sharing something of her own. It has caused Sally great angst and she does not know how to deal with it. The sad part is that she will never know if this girl is intentionally doing it, a kind of mean-girl strategy to intentionally ignore someone and socially isolate them, which is very common among high school girls. Or perhaps, she is simply not picking up the clues or is insecure about the attention that Sally (a pretty, vivacious and popular girl) gets. I helped Sally by encouraging her to come up with other alternate and more helpful interpretations of this 'friend's' behaviour, while recognizing for myself that this was a new facet for young people to deal with during adolescence. The insecurity of not knowing whether a subtle message was being given by someone or it was a matter of delay in the messaging app is an entirely new relationship drama that the Net Generation has to deal with.

I have been told by many young people that the blue ticks that WhatsApp has introduced to tell people whether their message has been read or not is very anxiety-provoking for young people. Since they are used to controlling their interactions and can pretend they did not see the message or were not on the phone (they can, after all, turn off the last seen feature on WhatsApp, much to the chagrin of many parents), they claim that the 'read' feature of WhatsApp causes them anxiety because if they have seen the message, they are expected to reply on time, and if they don't, there will be social repercussions for them.

3. Many young Net Geners, it seems, are aware that virtual intimacy is a poor substitute for the real thing. Some

research at UCLA, for example, shows that texting, the teenagers' increasingly preferred mode of communication with their friends, makes them feel less connected and bonded than face-to-face communication. This research showed that the closer the experience was to in-person conversation, the more emotionally connected the friends felt. People who communicated via video chat, for example, reported feeling a closer connection than those who telephoned, while those who used the phone found a closer connection than those who communicated via text.[14] This research suggests that when they do engage in more intense forms of communication, adolescents report more emotional satisfaction; yet at the same time, because the trend is towards privileging efficiency over intimacy, quantity over quality, most teens will communicate via text.

4. Close childhood friendships also lay the groundwork for healthy adult relationships, including intimate ones. By trying to sanitize relationships of all difficult emotions, the Net Generation may be losing the ability to connect on a deeper level. If the Net Generation is not trained in one-to-one communication, how are they going to deal with the messy intimacy that comes with interactions in relationships such as marriage?

5. You are connected 24/7, but to whom? While interviewing young people for this book, I was surprised at the strength of emotion showed by Melanie, a fourteen-year-old South Asian girl living in Europe. 'I hate the iPhone!' she declared. 'I want you to tell everyone that. I use it and go on it every day because that is what everyone does. My Dad said, "If you can't beat us, join us." It upsets me though. It angers me that at night, instead of talking to each other, my whole

family is glued to their screens. I want to throw all the phones out of the window. I wish we could talk to each other instead of to people all over the world.'

This young girl makes a very important point about the impact of technology on relationships. We are now expected to be available to all people at all times. As soon as the ping of a message comes, we feel compelled to see what it is immediately. The person on the other side of the message becomes the most important person in our lives at that time. Regardless of what we are doing or who we are with, we end up responding to the message instead of being present with those who are with us.

Children and teens today are also connected to more people than anyone from their parents' generation ever was. Yet, despite this age of easy connectivity, experts are raising the alarm on what this constant connectivity means for the Net Generation, and how it is not what it appears to be. By now, it is a cliché to say that we have never been 'connected' to so many people, thanks to the Internet. Diaspora families, in particular, extol the virtues of technology in helping them feel connected to families. Grandparents are grateful to be able to see their grandchildren on Skype and Facetime and be a regular part of their life, despite the geographical distance that separates them.

6. If you are typing hurtful messages and arguing over instant messaging, the emoticons do not really convey how your words are impacting the other person. Humans are unique and individual—reducing our expressions down to a formulaic palette of emoticons cannot even begin to capture the nuances and particularities of our internal responses. Technology also appears to have contributed to a disturbing

decrease in empathy amongst young adults. A University of Michigan study found that college students in 2012 scored 40 per cent less on empathy scales than a few decades ago, and a lower level of interest in other people or in trying to understand their perspective.[15] It seems that intimate relationships cannot be sanitized into neat little packages. If we try to avoid negative emotions, we lose a bit of our humanity with it. Human beings cannot selectively switch off emotions—if we attempt to do that, we will hamper joy as well as the pain that we seek to distance ourselves from. If we try to keep hurt at bay, we lose the joy as well as the pleasure. One wonders if the feeling of numbness, purposelessness and low-grade sadness that so many young people currently report feeling has anything to do with the depersonalizing of communication and relationships.

7. By being able to edit and reflect on what we send as messages—sometimes even showing them to other friends before sending them—we are able to control the amount of vulnerability we will experience and the amount of attention we will give the other. We manage to create the distance but then do not understand why our human heart feels so empty and sad. Most of us as adults have at least had it another way. Children today do not know any other way and, therefore, are less likely to understand what is missing. They feel a loneliness in their core which they cannot understand or articulate.

8. We live in a time when there is always more to do than time to do it in. More than ever, our time and attention has become our greatest treasures. When we are tethered to our devices in the company of loved ones, we are giving the gift of our time to everyone except those sitting or standing

right in front of us. Giving someone attention is a basic principle of relationship-building and intimacy, and more than that, acknowledges the basic worth of a human being. In a close relationship, the hurt one feels when attention is withdrawn can feel like physical pain—one of the signs of a failing relationship.

But the turning away of attention is becoming the norm in the age of technology. Paying attention to those around you, greeting them, making eye contact has been a basic sign of respect in many cultures. It is concerning that children who have grown up in the digital age find this too intense, too intimate.

Although dividing our attention may have become the norm, it does not mean that it does not upset or hurt those on the receiving end. Mary, a young university student, shared a story that brought tears to her eyes even months after it happened. She was at her high school graduation. Her final year had not been easy and it had taken a lot of perseverance to graduate on time. She was excited to see that her parents and siblings got a good seat from where they could view the proceedings. As her name was called and she stepped on to the stage, she glanced expectantly at her family in the gallery to wave to them—and noticed that her dad was looking at his BlackBerry rather than at her. Since the whole process of her walking up on to the stage, getting her diploma and walking off only took a few moments, her dad missed most of it. The fact that he had supported her throughout her life, was there on time, was a great father and the hero of her life was lost in the hurt she felt when he diverted his attention from her shining moment. When she later asked him who he was communicating with, he could not even remember! Responding to a text from an unimportant person spoilt what was one of the biggest moments of his daughter's life.

The question we need to ask ourselves is: who are we connected to all the time? Not to those closest to us. It is usually our loved ones who share physical space with us and it is they who are on the receiving end when we turn our attention away. What message does this give them? Parents born before the 1990s have experienced something different. We can recognize the difference between intimacy born of true human connection and flat, colourless attempts at intimacy mediated through technology. It would be sad, indeed, if the Net Generation lost out on tasting the simple joy that comes with truly connecting to another human being. And yet, that is exactly where they seem to be heading. Moreover, since relationships are the single biggest predictor of happiness, we need to take technology's impact on relationships seriously.

Encouraging good communication etiquette

❐ Encourage children to talk to people in person and on the telephone, rather than to simply text.

❐ Remind children to excuse themselves before answering a phone or texting in public.

❐ Encourage them to use respectful body language to show that they are listening to the other person present physically.

❐ Foster good communication skills by modelling them yourself and encouraging your children to follow.

❐ Encourage them to have unplugged time together in all their important relationships.

❐ Set an example that important messages should be communicated in person or via the phone, rather than texts, even if it is difficult and uncomfortable.

Chapter 7

Impact on the Soul

No behaviour problem is just the kid's problem; it's also a family problem. To help your child best, you need to step back and look at the big picture and ask, 'What are all the factors that might be causing my child to misbehave?'
—Dr Michele Borba

Parents at a drop-in group session had many concerns about the impact of media and technology on their children's value system and what they considered 'normal' and acceptable. Here are a few examples of what was shared:

Selina, a young professional mother, was more confused than distraught. 'I am a modern, professional and open-minded woman,' she began. 'I have had the sex talk with my older kids, *and* I use the correct terms for anatomy and everything,' she said, trying to convince me (and herself) that she was not a 'prude'. 'I have an open mind about sexuality and I am not ashamed of my body. In fact, the sexualized nature of society (which I accept as a fact beyond my control) is such that I had to have the talk with my children before they were really ready to understand it.

'Yet, when I look at the six-year-olds in my daughter's first grade class, I cannot help but react. They are not playing "pretend house" and "doctors", like we did as children. Their swinging hips and pouting lips suggest sexuality far beyond their years. Children have always played pretend grown-up games but now there is a seedy quality to their play. It's hard to express, yet it just feels wrong in the gut.'

Neesha, a high school teacher in a public school, recalled a costume party for middle school children in a middle class neighbourhood. 'Guess what the most popular outfit this year was?' she asked. 'A slut,' she replied, without waiting for us to answer. 'How are we to raise girls who respect themselves and set boundaries when this is who they want to be? How can we teach our boys to respect women when being a "slut" is the image that young women are aspiring to?'

'Buying clothes for my two young girls has always been a challenging exercise,' said another mom. 'I am continuously horrified at the sexualized clothing available for young girls, and at increasingly younger ages. Why would anyone want to dress their nine-year-old in a bustier or a thong? What message is that sending?'

Parents were desperately trying to understand what happened and how their children seemed to have fast-forwarded from being toddlers to these seductresses in children's bodies.

'It happened so suddenly that I am reeling. I expected to deal with issues around sexuality when they were teenagers. But one minute my child was a toddler and the next she was lip-synching and dancing to Miley Cyrus videos,' says the mother of a nine-year-old. 'To be honest, I am so used to it that most of the time, I don't notice. I zone out and live in my own world and tell myself that everyone her age is doing it. But now that you mention it, I worry that my child will think this is the norm. That there is nothing wrong with it.'

'I was disgusted at the story of Chris Brown beating his girlfriend,'[1] says a quiet father in the group. 'I have always tried to teach my girls that they deserve and should expect respect. My girls were in their early teens when this story first broke. I expected that his fans would boycott him. I was horrified to find out that instead of boycotting his live shows, young people continue to swarm to them. There was a series of tweets by young women begging to be beaten by Brown. Have we sunk to this?'

Misha, an elementary school teacher, shares that the vast majority of the nine-year-olds in her class play violent video games. 'If the class is not responding, all I need to do is mention video games and they will perk up. The favourite game in the class is "Call of Duty", an extremely graphic and violent game. The boys say they love it because it is so realistic, with guns and bombs and blood.'

It was clear that this was a hot issue for parents. They were struggling to teach values which seemed to be completely at odds with what the children were watching on their various screens. Research validates that being exposed to 'too much, too soon' is the 'wallpaper of children's lives',[2] the background for their growing up. In the report presented to the Parliament of the United Kingdom, the researchers found that 90 per cent of parents agreed with the statement that there is too much pressure for children to grow up too fast.[3] I would add that it is growing up in inappropriate ways. There seems to be no indication that children are growing up too fast in terms of taking responsibility for their lives. In fact, the opposite seems to be true as is evidenced by phrases such as 'thirty is the new eighteen' and the 'boomerang generation', indicating that many see that children are taking longer to accept responsibility for their lives. The pressure to grow up is in early sexualization and in consumerism—both pressures, although building up in the last century, have been turbocharged by technology.

Pornography

Exposure to sexually explicit material for children can happen in one of two ways. The child is accidentally exposed to the image while looking for something else, or he intentionally goes looking for it. Both appear to be increasingly common. In a study of adolescents about sexual behaviours and attitudes, almost a 1,000 male participants (66 per cent) and more than one-third (39 per cent) of females had seen at least one sexually explicit posting in the past year.[4] It seems that parents are frequently unaware when their child has been exposed to sexually explicit material. In the 'Letting children be children' survey, 41 per cent of parents of children who *had* been exposed denied that such exposure had taken place, indicating that their children had either not told the parents of accidental exposure or that they had hidden intentional searches for pornography.[5] In either case, a significant proportion of parents did not know what their child had been exposed to online. In light of the current climate, we can assume that many of our children have been or will be exposed to pornography even if we instal the best state-of-the-art filter software on our computers.

Exposure to pornography for children can have significant side effects. A study showed that early exposure to pornography for boys predicted that they would have a less than respectful attitude towards women and were more likely to perpetuate sexual harassment and engage in risky sexual behaviour.[6] For girls, childhood exposure to pornography also predicted less progressive gender roles and underage sexual activity.[7] Additionally, because it gives a distorted view of relationships, it may make young women more susceptible to not setting boundaries in relationships or recognizing unhealthy relationships.[8] In my own practice, I have noticed that young adults who view pornography have skewed ideas about normal sexual behaviour and have unrealistic expectations of sexual activity. They tend to believe that what they see on the screen is 'proper sex' and find their own intimate lives unexciting by comparison. They often confuse Hollywood and Bollywood and marital sex. It is clear that watching sexualized images in childhood has the effect of making them seem 'normal' and conveys unhealthy attitudes towards women in particular.

For parents, in addition to doing what we can to protect our children from viewing such images, it is also important to counteract these messages with our own value-based ones. Given the messages that media is putting out there, we cannot assume that our children can discern right from wrong or can make judgements about healthy sexuality. If we do not speak up, ours will be the only voice missing in the cacophony of voices pressuring them to grow up before they are ready.

The erosion of values

The participants in the parenting group seemed a bit sceptical when I suggested that our children were having a crisis of conscience and that media was contributing to the erosion of values. A couple of parents suggested that it was perhaps giving media too much power. I found that research validated my hunch.

A recent study published in *Cyberpsychology: Journal of Psychosocial Research on Cyberspace* presented some truly disturbing findings.[9] In attempting to link the change in values to media and technology for pre-teen children aged from nine to eleven, the researchers analyzed values presented in popular TV shows in North America. They found that between the 1960s and 1990s, popular TV shows like *Happy Days*, *Growing Pains* and *Sabrina the Teenage Witch* displayed values like community feeling, tradition and benevolence, among the healthy values. The shows also glorified popularity and image. By the early 2000s, the top five values displayed in popular TV shows were fame, achievement, popularity, image and financial success. It is no surprise, then, that the top goal listed by 81 per cent of young people today is 'getting rich'. The values that were least displayed were spiritualism, tradition, security, conformity, benevolence and community feeling. The study also found that the vast majority of TV shows for this age group were about young people who find fame and stardom with little effort and few setbacks.[10]

An expert in media psychology, Dimitri A. Christakis explains how what children see on screen gets imbedded into their subconscious mind and normalizes it for them.[11] Christakis says that when children are watching television, there is a significant change in the electrical circuitry within the brain. The state of the brain, he explains, changes from an alert state (beta waves) to a hypnotic state (alpha waves). When this happens, what is presented bypasses the prefrontal cortex of the brain or the 'judgement centre' and implants itself into the deep unconscious area of the brain. In other words, there is no real opportunity for the child to decipher whether what is being shown is right or wrong.[12] The alpha state is a great learning state where learning is automatic and easy, but when what is presented is violence and pornography, it also gets learnt easily and automatically.

Since parents are also impacted by media, it is hard for us to look at it objectively. I invite you to sit down and watch a TV programme with your children. Do not comment but look at it from the point of view of the value messages the programme is sending. If we can go beyond the beautiful graphics, sound effects and witty dialogue, we may discern values contrary to what we would like our children to imbibe. When we recognize that our children are unconsciously absorbing all these messages, it becomes clear that an unfettered media diet is not recommended.

Television is not the only medium that sends value-toxic messages to youth. The celebrity culture, which glorifies rule-breaking by giving it attention on social media, sends the message that it is glamorous to be above the law. Role models like Lindsay Lohan and Chris Brown do not see any negative impact on their popularity when they make poor decisions. This trend is also present in the athletic world when role models for children turn out hollow; for example, some have used drugs to enhance their performance, such as Lance Armstrong. Research has shown that when society holds a high standard of morality, there is a contagious effect on others, who will be 'contained' by society's standards and not act on their unethical urges. When unethical or immoral behaviour becomes accepted and normalized, it encourages those who would be contained in a more ethical environment to act out their unethical urges.[12]

Sexting

Sexting is one of the latest trends amongst young people that is causing much concern to parents. It involves sending a sexually explicit text message or photograph (either nude or topless) to someone else via a cell phone. The dangers inherent in such behaviour would seem almost too obvious to mention, yet it appears that up to 25 per cent of teens have engaged in sending a sexually explicit photograph.[13] This percentage goes further up if sexually explicit texts not involving pictures are taken into account. According to statistics reported by GuardChild, as many as 39 per cent of teens admitted to sending suggestive text messages.[14]

Why would adolescents do this? Teens suggest various reasons for Sexting, including flirting with someone they 'want to hook up with', wanting to be cool, giving a signal that they were ready to go to the next level with the person, or in response to pressure put upon them by their partner. As expected, more girls than boys are pressurized to engage in Sexting, usually by a present or potential boyfriend.[15]

Although some teens have always engaged in risky sexual behaviour, Sexting is particularly worrisome because of the ease with which the message can be sent and since there is no real way of destroying the message once the sender has pressed 'send'. Adolescent relationships are notoriously fickle and to engage in a sexual exchange with someone who can make it go 'viral' is making one vulnerable. A moment of throwing caution to the wind may hound the young person for many years to come and potentially impact her chances at employment, relationships and further education.

Even the person responsible for forwarding a Sext sent to them in trust is not immune from significant repercussions. A less talked about concern with Sexting is that it is illegal in many jurisdictions and there are many stories of children being criminally charged for sending messages containing nude pictures. The highly publicized case of P. Alpert, a Florida native, is a case in point. This eighteen-year-old boy's girlfriend broke up with him and to take revenge, he forwarded a Sext sent by his then girlfriend to her friends and family. He ended up with a criminal conviction and his name was placed on the sex offenders registry for twenty-five years.[16] One can only imagine the emotional and mental cost to this young person of a flash of anger when he tried to get back at his girlfriend.

Snapchat

The newest instant messaging tool on the block (at the time of writing) is Snapchat. Children and teens love it because it appears to circumvent the issue of digital footprints by self-destroying after a few seconds. This generation is slowly coming to the realization that you cannot share on SNSs like Facebook because of the permanence and because too many adults are watching. They prefer to use apps like Snapchat because the content is ephemeral, so it removes inhibitions about sharing. According to interview reports, its founders created the multibillion-dollar app because they knew that lots of people regretted sending messages on their phone. Although this is what makes the app attractive to youngsters and popular for Sexting, many children I spoke to said that they 'know friends' who can save the images of Snapchat. Others with nimble fingers can take screenshots before the image goes away.

For parents trying to teach values to children, it is worrisome that what makes Snapchat so popular is the 'no accountability' of the medium with no digital footprints. It appears to encourage its users to let go of inhibitions as well as fear of consequences and Snapchat away with reckless abandon. The problem is that fear of consequences is a very important part of our emotional and ethical make-up that stops us from wrongdoing even if we may be angry or upset. It is like taking away police surveillance—some people may continue to drive carefully, but there will be a significant percentage that are only deterred by the fear that they may be caught by the police. Regardless of parental concerns, Snapchat seems to be one of the favourite apps of children at present. By June 2013, Snapchat was sharing 350 million pictures a day![17] Its popularity has given rise to apps like Snapchat and Hack which circumvent the privacy features of the app and allow people to share pictures, bringing the issue of digital footprints and sharing again to the forefront.

Violence

Discussions rage about the impact of watching violence on screens and its effect on children and their developing brains. It is estimated that before age eighteen, the average child who watches regular TV will have witnessed 200,000 acts of violence on TV, including 16,000 murders.[18] It appears that there are two main ways in which a child's brain can cope with watching violence and neither appear conducive to maintaining emotional and spiritual health.

Research confirms that like watching pornography, accessing

violent material also has an impact on children's emotional well-being and behaviour.[19] The various studies point to an increase in aggression, impulsive behaviour, lack of empathy and desensitization to violence, among other effects. A study by Dimitri Christakis and Frederick Zimmerman found that boys who watched violent television programmes at young ages were at risk for behavioural problems at ages seven to ten.[20]

We are the first generation in the history of our planet to be continuously and persistently bombarded with wanton violence in onscreen programmes, virtually participating in it and even getting rewarded for conducting violence in video games. There is some evidence that children today are desensitized to such violence and graphic images.[21] I believe the desensitization to the violence is directly linked to the numbing of empathy in a child's brain. Human beings are hard-wired for empathy and even babies have been shown to display it for other babies and to comfort them when they are crying. When a child is exposed to violence, the natural impulse is to want to help the person. The brain has to override this spiritual human impulse to show compassion and to help the other—has to disengage to protect itself. The problem is that you cannot selectively numb empathy. The brain has to dial down all emotions, 'put a blanket on them', so to speak, in order to cope with the impact on the emotions and the senses.

If the brain is not able to protect itself, persistently being exposed to violence is likely to cause trauma. For example, there are many reports of how people who work in crime and policing and forensics are often traumatized by what they see.[22] They have to deal with the emotional fall-out from being exposed to the violence that destroys lives. They probably have access to counselling and psychological support that helps them through what they experience—so it is a sad commentary on human evolution today that the material these crime-fighting officers find traumatic is available on the Internet and is accessible by millions, including children. One can only wonder at the long-term emotional and spiritual impact on these young souls who witness violence not in the context of a job or serving humanity, but simply as voyeurs to see the next weird thing on YouTube.

Trauma

When I was facilitating a trauma group for women, a young woman in her thirties mentioned that her anxiety started when she was very young as she tried to sleep while her parents watched TV. She mentioned that she had never articulated to her parents what the sounds of gunshots, bombs and people wailing and screaming did to her. Her parents, well-meaning and good parents by all accounts, had no idea of the silent terror she suffered night after night. After she shared her story, two other women came forward with similar stories. Granted this was a group of women suffering from various forms of trauma and, therefore, more sensitive to such factors, but it got me thinking about how children are often in the same space as others watching violence and sexuality and the impact it would have on their brains, which are not able to distinguish virtual from real life.

Misha, an elementary schoolteacher shares that the vast majority of the nine-year-olds in her class play video games. While not all video games are violent, many of the most popular ones, such as 'Call of Duty', 'Modern Warfare' and 'Black Ops' are. The violence in these games have been linked to copycat violence in children and teens. The American Academy of Child and Adult Psychiatry notes that children who are consistently exposed to this kind of violence on the video game screens become more desensitized to violence in real life and are more likely to use violence to deal with everyday problems.[23] A study published by the *Journal of Pediatrics* cautioned paediatricians about the potential outcomes of a violent media diet, which are aggressive behaviour, desensitization to violence, nightmares and fear. The article warns paediatricians that the issue is so significant that questioning children about their media habits at well child clinics is warranted![24]

There is the famous story about frogs which goes something like this: although the scientific basis of the metaphor has sometimes been questioned, the premise is that if you put a frog into a pan of boiling water, the frog's self-defence mechanism will kick in and it will jump out to save itself. However, if you put the same frog in cold water and then very gradually heat up the water, the frog will not recognize the rising temperature until it is too late. It will slowly be desensitized to the change and be boiled alive.

The same is true of human beings. When we are faced with obvious danger, we rush to protect ourselves and our children. However, when the norms of society change and we become desensitized to the pollution of our psyche and our souls, we take no steps to protect ourselves until it is too late.

Reflection points for parents

- ❏ Become aware of the value-based messages that your children are unconsciously ingesting.
- ❏ Encourage them to become more conscious and critical of messages in media.
- ❏ Communicate and discuss the matter with your children after they view something that might be upsetting to them.

Part 3

STEPS TO THRIVING AS A FAMILY IN THE DIGITAL AGE

Chapter 8

Danger and Safety in Cyberspace

I personally like to think of the Internet as a parallel universe, a cyber-world as opposed to the real-world. In the cyber-world people do much the same thing as in the real-world, such as chat, work, or go shopping. And, as in the real-world, there are dangers. In the real-world, we spend years as children learning about the world and all its dangers before we can safely go out on our own. This is not the case in cyber-world. People wander into cyber-world as cyber-toddlers or even cyber-infants. How can these people be expected to look after themselves in this strange new world?...I believe that education must be the first step to computer security. The cyber-world is too complex and dangerous to jump into without understanding the dangers.
—Jimi Loo, in Comments and Feedback to Noam Eppel's article, 'Security Absurdity: The Complete, Unquestionable, and Total Failure of Information Security. A long-overdue wake up call for the security community.'

We have been discussing the long-term impact of technology on various aspects of our children's well-being. In this chapter, we talk about the immediate safety issues for children while they are online. Some schools do give children basic safety guidelines for safe net navigation but few parents are similarly educated, unless they look for such information themselves. Research shows that although parents may be vaguely aware of the dangers that lurk in the online world, they consistently underestimate the immediate threat to their own children. Additionally, when children have been exposed to various threats online, the vast majority do not tell their parents about it.

It is important to note that not all children are vulnerable on the Internet. Well-adjusted children who have active offline lives and close relationships with trusted adults are the least vulnerable. Children with low self-esteem, other mental health issues, troubled relationships and an unmet longing for love and attention are most at risk in virtual space.

Also, there are many more healthy friendships formed on the Internet than unhealthy ones. Not all children experience inappropriate behaviour online; many have mostly positive experiences and form healthy relationships. Therefore, a balanced and realistic view of the virtual world is essential. Having said that, the dangers are very real and significant. We must be aware of them and train our children in basic safety protocol so that they can continue to have positive and balanced online experiences.

There are three main dangers that children are at risk of being exposed to:

1. Sexual solicitation
2. Cyberbullying
3. Loss of privacy—digital footprints and identity theft

Sexual solicitation and predators

Both digital and traditional print media today are full of stories of Internet-related paedophilia scandals. These are sensational stories and fodder for the media, which gives a lot of airtime to such stories because they validate the fears that parents already have for their children.

Parental fear for children's safety is not new, of course. Before the Internet age, parents used to warn their children about talking to strangers and being suspicious of people they did not know. In the pre-digital age, it became apparent that the vast majority of children who experienced sexual violence or abuse did so at the hands of those they knew and whom the parents trusted, such as a relative or family friend, so safety measures by parents were often ineffective.

Alarm signals to keep children safe from paedophiles have been magnified several hundredfold since the Internet has come into our homes. It has provided potential offenders unprecedented access to children in the safety of their homes. Parents can no longer be certain that their children are safe in the sanctity of their own homes. The Internet has also made many would-be offenders much bolder and at times 'normalized' their perversions because they can find online communities which validate their respective perversions and encourage them. In an interview with MSNBC, the American television network, former US customs agent Marcus Lawson said, 'I don't think the Internet has created more paedophiles. It's removed the societal stigma that kind of kept people in check. Before the net, paedophilia was a lonely business. Now twenty-four hours a day, seven days a week, you can validate yourself, find hundreds and hundreds of people who will tell you there's nothing wrong with having sex with children.'[1]

Today, there are thousands of cases of Internet-related child-luring tracked by the National Center for Missing and Exploited Children in the USA and according to some surveys, one in five children confessed that they had received a sexual solicitation online.[2]

Parents sometimes believe that young adolescents and curious children may invite sexual predators if they search for pornography online. Experts, however, say that the biggest threat to children comes not from what comes into the children's computers but what goes out. What this means is that although children watching pornography may be harmed in other ways, the danger of sexual solicitation comes through the sites that children roam in cyberspace and what they share. The biggest threat to children, perhaps, is people who lurk in chat rooms and Internet Relay Chat (IRC) channels who actively solicit children with the aim of luring them into having online sex or a face-to-face meeting.[3] IRCs are interest-based virtual chat rooms that enable users to connect to a network of IRC servers. Because of the anonymity of users and the use of screen names rather than real names, interactions in IRC rooms tend to be less inhibited than other types of exchanges on the Internet. It is also much easier to be deceived by the identity of the other person. Additionally, IRC rooms tend to be male-dominated, with aggression and bad language accepted and frequent. Although some children do use IRCs, it is a dangerous environment not at all suited to them.

To maintain safety on the Internet, it is best to ensure that children stay away from IRC chat rooms. If a child is very eager to go on chat rooms for a particular hobby or interest, it is essential that he does so only with active parental supervision.

Cyberbullying

Cyberbullying is the use of digital technology to repeatedly harm or harass other people in a deliberate manner. According to US Legal Definitions: 'Cyber-bullying could be limited to posting rumors or gossips about a person in the Internet bringing about hatred in other's minds; or it may go to the extent of personally identifying victims and publishing materials severely defaming and humiliating them.'[4]

With the proliferation of Internet access, cyberbullying has become a common occurrence with the Net Generation. There have been some highly publicized, sad cases of children committing suicide because they could not show their faces to peers after being vilified online. One such case was the suicide of Tyler Clementi, a student at Rutgers University. Tyler jumped off a bridge after his roommate videotaped him meeting another man and published it on social media.[5]

Suicide attempts are not unheard of among victims of cyberbullying. While every case is not tragic, cyberbullying is potentially very damaging to children and can affect self-esteem, causing anger, frustration and a variety of other emotional and psychological problems in the victim.[6] It can also result in school delinquency as the victims may not want to face their peers. Other reactions are substance abuse and antisocial behaviour as the victim tries to cope with the bullying.[7]

Studies show that cyberbullying seems to be on the increase and that older adolescents (over fourteen years) tend to experience it more frequently than younger users, maybe because they tend to go on the Internet more often and unsupervised.[8]

The 2004 I-Safe.org survey of 1,500 students in the fourth to eighth grades found that 42 per cent of all children have been bullied while they were online.[9] Other surveys put the figure at a lower percentage.[10] A quarter of those have been bullied repeatedly.[11] The mean and hurtful messages come via email or text.[12]

It is very important for parents to be aware of the fact that fewer than 15 per cent of children who experience cyberbullying tell their parents about it.[13] This may be one reason why so many parents deny that their children have been bullied while the children confess that they have.

Therefore, parents must be watchful if their child suddenly changes her computer behaviour, or shows signs of mood changes or changes in eating and sleeping patterns. While not conclusively indicative of cyberbullying, these changes in mood and behaviour need to be investigated by parents to rule out technology-related harassment. Of course, it is also important to train children not to engage in mean or hurtful behaviour online themselves, as 58 per cent of children in the survey admitted to saying mean or hurtful things to others.[14]

Experts have been trying to understand why cyberbullying has become so common. Here are some possible hypotheses:

1) Unlike face-to-face bullying, a cyberbully can hide his identity quite easily, thereby escaping consequences. Given that bullying is primarily engaged in by youth who may be called cowards, cyberbullying is particularly suited to children who do not have the courage to face the victim.

2) It is easier to be cruel with the use of technology because the impact on the victim is not visible.[15] The distance means the bully does not see the psychological harm being caused to the victim.

3) The hurtful actions of a cyberbully can be widely public as many others can add to the harm by forwarding mean information or rumours about the victim.

4) Since many parents do not keep a strict eye on their children's online activities, they can miss the actions of the bully and the impact on the victim.

5) Even if parents do find out, many report that it is challenging to determine the right course of action. They are confused about whether to confront the bully's family or not, for example.

What you should do if your child is being bullied

1. Believe your children, do not suggest that they contributed to the problem and get them emotional support, if necessary. Get their view on the issue and ask them what they would like do about it. Many children may not be ready to tale tattle on their peers, so parents need to recognize this and talk them through it, explaining that if not stopped, the bully may continue to victimize others.

2. Gather proof: keep records of conversations and messages that are inappropriate.
3. Contact the school and inform the authorities. Many schools have policies against bullying and will take action.
4. Do not contact the parents of the bully directly.
5. Report the incident to the relevant platform. For example, if it happens on Facebook or Twitter, contact the social media platform and insist that they take action against the offender.
6. Block the offender.

Stopping your child from bullying

1. Continuously reinforce values of respect for others, foster empathy, compassion and right perspectives.
2. Encourage your children to speak up when they witness bullying. Bystanders have an important role to play in either stopping or continuing bullying.
3. Have a zero tolerance policy for bullying at home.

Loss of privacy

> *'If you have something that you don't want anyone to know, maybe you shouldn't be doing it in the first place.'*
> —Eric Schmidt, past CEO of Google, in an interview with the CNBC network.[16]

This quote from the then CEO of Google may sound a bit arrogant but it reflects the new age that we are living in. Privacy appears to be dead. Once you post something online, you have no control over where and how it will travel on the Internet. One can argue that the spreading of information is the risk that we take in living in a connected world. Of course, it is not always true that the only control you have over your information is before you put it online, as we will see. There are thousands of instances where people post information or pictures of other people, thereby compromising their privacy without any choice or action on their part.

This is especially troubling for children. Many would agree that youth is a time to try new things, a time for making and learning from mistakes. To grow into successful and healthy adults, children need to be held accountable for their mistakes and experience consequences of their actions. However, they do need some leeway, an assurance that their youthful indiscretions will not be held against them forever. Many young people report posting things they later regret. 'What was I thinking?' they might remark. They may take pictures of themselves doing things or visiting places which, in hindsight, are inappropriate. They may send a message or picture in the heat of an emotion which, upon reflection, turns out to be a bad idea. Of course, the click-happy nature of the online world makes it extremely easy to post things without thinking and the online culture actually encourages it. The co-developer of Snapchat, Evan Spiegel, is reported to have said that they want to keep shrinking the time it takes to having an experience and sharing it.[17] This kind of thinking and environment is putting a lot of strain on young children's still-developing self-control muscles. Unlike when we parents were growing up, today's mistakes by children are likely to haunt them far into their future, perhaps impacting their chances at careers and relationships long after the regretful incident is over. Children may repent a moment of indiscretion but the digital footprints are firm. The Internet does not forget.

This is how celebrities have always lived, a stream of paparazzi following their every move. And we have heard and read about the kind of pressure it puts on them when their whole life is on display.[18] The same thing happens when a person stands for office and, for example, his past is open for investigation. In the digital age, anyone with an Internet connection has access to information. This is not to make parents more paranoid than they already are; it is simply to alert us to the possible consequences of our actions.

Parents are at least as culpable as children in this regard, sometimes more so. Statistics show that people with children are more likely to use social media, especially to post pictures of their children. In a survey conducted by print site www.posterista.co.uk, 2,367 parents of children aged five and under were surveyed to discover the way parents share information and images of their children. The recent survey found that an astounding 94 per cent of parents in the United Kingdom have posted pictures on their children online, mostly on Facebook, Flickr and Instagram.[19] This figure is substantially higher than a 2011 survey, which had asked relatively older parents (those born in the 1960s and '70s) about their picture posting habits. In that survey, 66 per cent of parents reported posting pictures of their children online and the majority also said that they shared children's accomplishments on social media, such as school and sports achievements and awards.[20] Other reports from various jurisdictions around the world also suggest that the vast majority of parents share their children's pictures online without giving much thought to the digital footprint that their children will inherit.[21]

While information that children post themselves is sometimes problematic, the pictures that parents post open the door to other kinds of dangers, such as data and identity theft.

There are various concerns about posting information about our children online. Firstly is the social and psychological impact on the child, since sharing happens without the consent of the child who may have to live with the consequences forever.

Parents need to be mindful of what they share and this is not easy because there are huge commercial and economic forces out there whose bottom line and profit depend upon how much people share. They use their vast financial backing to subtly (and not so subtly) influence the mindsets of people to encourage them to share.[22]

The dangers of giving out too much information online is that in the wrong hands, it can be used to steal yours or your child's identity. As seasoned identity thieves remark, it is easier than ever to steal identities. If they have access to a person's date of birth, location and a passport picture, they are well on their way to having enough information to build a fake identity.[23]

What parents need to do

- ❏ Repeatedly highlight the fact that any information your children post online can go public.
- ❏ Emphasize that all information is public by default. If you do nothing to prevent it, all your information is available to whoever desires to access or use it.
- ❏ Go through the security features of social media accounts together with your children and make sure that they are set to high privacy settings. Because these security settings are subject to change, set aside time on a monthly basis to review what has changed and adjust accordingly.
- ❏ Remind everyone in the family not to share passport or credit card information on any website without the express permission of at least one parent. This permission needs to be granted on a case-by-case basis.

The next few chapters lay out a five-step plan to manage technology within our families so that our family can thrive in the digital age.

Chapter 9

Step 1: Get Your Own Act Together

*What you are doing speaks so loudly that I cannot hear
what you are saying.*
—Anonymous

As a parent, how you live your life has an impact on your
children. As the old parenting adage goes, do not be upset that
your child is not listening to what you are saying but be aware
that they are watching everything that you are doing. Often, we
look at our child and see our reflection, a 'mini me'. In the
1970s, psychologist Albert Bandura developed *The Social
Learning Theory* noting that children learn social cues and
behaviours by observing the interactions of those around them.[1]
It is no surprise, then, that they appear to be acting like mini
versions of ourselves.

It is for this reason we really need to take a hard look at our
own relationship with technology. This, of course, is the hardest
part of disciplining our children because it is so much easier to
set limits for children than to look at our own actions. Many of
us struggle with our own relationship to technology while
trying to teach our children to be conscious of their bond to
their devices. And yet, this is exactly what we must do because it
is possibly the most effective discipline tool we have.

Tina is a case in point. She came to the group with an
iPhone in one hand and a baby carrier in the other, with her
toddler following behind, begging to play on the iPad. Tina was
frustrated because she could not get Lina, a talkative and friendly
young girl, to give up the device without a tantrum. During the
session, Tina realized that not only was she showing a very

unhealthy attachment to technology, but was also frequently distracted by her devices. To Tina's credit, she decided to get her own act together before trying to manage her toddler's growing addiction. A few weeks later, she reported that it was probably the hardest thing she remembers doing, ranked high up there with quitting smoking. She remarked that although she had not yet started to address Lina's addiction, the toddler seemed calmer, happier and less attached to her devices.

The change in behaviour that Lina exhibited is not surprising at all. In addition to the messages that she was getting through Tina's change in behaviour, she was also responding to the fact that her mother was emotionally available and more present for her.

So although this chapter is about setting an example, we are going to start by talking about parental distraction, when parents are physically present but mentally and emotionally unavailable. Our own addiction to our devices means giving our children and our families fragmented attention. It is important to point out that parental distraction has wider implications than simply impacting our children's relationship with technology.[2]

A few years ago, a child's death made international headlines: A three-month-old baby girl named Sarang (meaning love in Korean) died of malnutrition while her parents spent their time at an Internet café caring for a virtual child named Anima.[3]

Internet cafés had recently sprung up all over Korea as an outcome of rapid economic growth, and Internet companies made it easy for those who could not afford an Internet connection at home to spend online time in a neighbourhood café at a low price. Sarang's parents met online, got together in real life and had a real-life child. It seems they did not know how to take care of a real baby, as she did not flash lights or signal that she needed to be fed and cuddled. The CNN reporter who broke the story suggested that they were not bad parents as such, just clueless. They would come home, feed the baby and go back to gaming for twelve-hour stretches until one day, they came home from a gaming session to find the baby had died of severe malnutrition.[4]

Although the story did not say that apart from malnutrition, the child could have died of a lack of emotional sustenance, since she was deprived of nurturing human contact for long periods.

Let us now consider a less extreme example from my clinical practice. Jenny is a mild, well-meaning mom in her early forties who came for therapy due to marital issues and the stress of having a child later on in life. Jenny confessed that she had become very distracted lately because of stress in her marital relationship. She said that she felt lonely and yearned for adult company while caring for her toddler, which is why she is online more frequently than she intends to. Last week, while she was feeding her toddler, she was simultaneously checking her WhatsApp messages. She found herself getting annoyed at the toddler when he disrupted her reading of a particularly funny message. She was engrossed in watching a video clip when she glanced down and saw that her baby was choking. She was horrified that although the baby was in her lap at the time, she was so distracted that she did not notice he had momentarily stopped breathing. She said that she still got flashbacks of what could have happened.

She is not alone. Injuries due to distracted parenting are becoming increasingly common. The Centre for Disease Control (CDC) links many everyday childhood injuries to distracted parenting, when parents are distracted by their devices.[5]

Another mother confesses that she is hooked on 'Fruit Ninja', an easy game that her son put on her iPad because he thought a non-techie like her could play it. She reported that she is unable to stop playing additional rounds of the one-minute game, to the detriment of her daily chores. On her way back from work, she finds herself looking forward to sitting down on the couch and begin playing her game. She is both proud of and somewhat embarrassed about her high score, which is even better than her children's, she claims.

It is crucial to understand how important focused attention from parents is for children. Paying positive attention to our children when they are very young is one of the most effective things we can do as parents to set them up for success in later life.[6] We know that physical touch is vital to a child's physical development, but a child deprived of a loving touch will fail to thrive, as is shown in many studies done in orphanages around the world.[7] Other research has pointed to how babies are primed to gaze into their mother's eyes as soon as their eyes can focus. This eye contact provides babies with a vital bonding experience and makes them feel safe.[8]

Bonding and attachment to a parent or primary caregiver is equally vital for a child's mental, emotional and social development. Attachment research shows that when a parent directs her attention to a baby in a positive way, the baby forms a secure base from where to explore the world.[9] Attention to a young child, then, is like psychological air: just as the human brain is damaged without oxygen, a baby's emotional brain cannot thrive without attention from a caregiver.

Only now is research being done to measure parental distraction caused by technology. In a recent small pilot study by the Boston Medical Center, Dr Jenny Radesky and her colleagues secretly observed fifty-five families eating out in restaurants; forty of those fifty-five used a cell phone during the meal. Many of the children of these forty families made escalating bids for attention during the meal and some of the parents responded with irritation at being interrupted in their virtual world. The study concluded that for the distracted parents, their 'primary engagement was with the device, rather than the child.'[10]

I suggest that you do some informal observing of your own. The next time you are in a public place, notice how much time parents and caregivers spend absorbed in their digital devices while children around them make repeated bids for attention. You will likely see many a parent absently push their stroller around while repeatedly tending to their iPhone. Just this week, I noticed a dad walking with two boys aged about five and seven. He was on the phone while the two little boys tried to first make silly faces, sing songs and then finally begin to hit each other in an attempt to get their father's attention. He, of course, got irritated and 'shushed' them, annoyed that his call was being disturbed. He only ended up with crying boys in a no-win situation.

It seems that even the very young recognize when their parents are distracted. In a study of six- to twelve-year-olds, children were asked if their parents were ever distracted and a whopping 62 per cent said yes, citing the cell phone as the most frequent cause of distraction.[11] It is interesting that a 2011 poll by Nielsen, the global information and measurement company, found that people with children use social media more than those without.[12] There are various theories about why this is so. Perhaps parents engage with social media to post pictures of their children, to connect with other parents on parenting issues. For some parents, being at home could give them a sense of parenting well by their mere presence, so they give themselves permission to browse social media. Children, homes and families take much work and looking after. It can be a lonely job which can feel unappreciated as well. Additionally, we cannot be expected to be focused on our children 24/7 which, by the way, is not good for them either. What we do need to prioritize as parents, however, is to be frequently emotionally and mentally available to them without technology vying for our attention.

It will be some time before longitudinal results about the full impact of technology-induced parental distraction is available, but by the time those studies are available, it will be too late for a whole generation of our children.

What I am not recommending here is to be hyper-vigilant and continuously focused on children. In fact, a certain amount of intentional 'looking the other way', benign neglect if you will, is good for children. They learn to entertain themselves, cope with frustration and solve problems. The difference is that such looking away is an intentional strategy to teach children vital life skills. It is not the unconscious distraction of being glued to our devices.

Here are some disturbing examples from my practice and various parent groups. Each of these children are saying what thousands experience on a daily basis.

Shamil's dad is an international banker who heads a regional division. Shamil is angry at his dad because he cannot switch off his 'crackberry' and is always preoccupied with work-related messages. Shamil recently screamed, 'Why don't you buy me an iPad, then maybe I can communicate with you!' The well-meaning dad completely missed the point of this tirade and actually bought the son an iPad—but was unable to comprehend why their relationship did not improve!

An older son and dad are having a conversation. The dad seems to be genuinely concerned when I overhear the son making a comment about his academic struggles. The dad asks a question but before the child can finish his answer, he looks down at his phone with a smile on his face, a highly inappropriate emotional reaction to the son's sharing of his struggles. The son sighs dejectedly and says, 'I guess we can finish this conversation later', to which the dad replies guiltily, 'No, no, I am listening. Go on. It's just that I am expecting an important email from work.'

We, as parents, tell ourselves that we need to spend quality time with our children, that some day we will schedule a tiny sliver of time when we *will* be present, with no distractions. The trouble is that the daily dose of distracted attention weakens the parent–child bond so much that by the time the quality time slot appears, there is already a conflict. We need to recognize that parenting, like other laws of nature, cannot be hurried—we need to slow down, be present for a significant quantity of time before any magic moments happen. The 'magic moments of parenting', sparkling times when we experience joy with our children because of a shared moment of connection, cannot be scheduled. They appear in the mundane, everyday routines when we are connected and emotionally available for our children.

The presence of the family in one location carrying out their own pursuits is not necessarily a bad thing—for generations, children have done their homework while Mom and Dad read the newspaper, prepared meals or chatted. The experience of being part of the family was a communal one, a group experience rather than necessarily one of 'quality time'. The difference with being distracted by technology, however, is that when people are online, they retreat into a virtual world which appears to fulfil their social needs. Connecting to others in the virtual world is an individual experience and appears less messy than real life connections to family members who may be demanding or bickering about mundane issues. We appear to be more in control of our online interactions. When we are so engrossed, however, the 'sixth sense' that parents have—eyes in the back of their heads, the parental instincts—seems to deteriorate. The more time we spend online, the worse our real life relationships get, further sending us to the virtual world and perpetuating the cycle of absentee parenting.

Mental health issues of children and adolescents

There is no doubt that mental health issues among the youth in North America are at an all-time low.[13] The HERI (Higher Education Research Institute) conducted a survey of over 200,000 students at 279 colleges and universities in the USA in 2010 and found that the mental and emotional well-being (happiness) of students is lower than it has been in at least three decades, when they first started gathering data.[14] Almost half (48 per cent) of students rated their own emotional health as 'below average', indicating that they expected to be happier than they were or that they perceived their peers to be.[15] In another survey of college counsellors, the American Psychological Association (APA) Monitor, a full 95 per cent of college counsellors said that anxiety, depression and relationship issues are rampant amongst college students and a significant cause of concern.[16]

Dr Ron Taffel, a highly respected family therapist and parent educator, believes that 'interrupted attention', which is the hallmark of today's parenting, is at least partly to blame for this epidemic of mental health issues.[17] He says that it is not as if today's parents are absent: no, in fact, they are very dedicated and more armed with information on how to successfully parent (thanks to technology) than ever before.[18] This fact was reiterated in my parent group where many mothers said that one factor that helps them parent better is all the information on child-rearing that is readily available online. Dr Taffel believes that although parents today know parenting theories well, they are not 'attuned' to their children because they are distracted and continuously shifting attention from child to 'away-from-child'.[19] I believe that the full impact of this 'there and not there parenting' is only just beginning to surface and we will not know the extent of the impact until it is too late. Add to this that it is much easier, in the short term, to connect through devices than in person, it further tempts us to turn to the conflict-free world of technology rather than deal with our own imperfect families.

Posting pictures

In the USA, a recent study found that 63 per cent of mothers use Facebook and among those who do, an astonishing 97 per cent share pictures of their children online, two-thirds share updates about what their children have done (accomplishments, birthdays, graduations and so on), and almost half of them share videos.[20] It seems harmless enough until you realize that given the rate at which the Internet world is emerging, changing and developing, we have no idea how and when these images and details may be used and for what. If we are choosing to post children's pictures online, there is definitely a risk in the present and an unknown but likely increasing risk in the future. There is simply too much at stake to take such a risk.

A brief look at one's newsfeed on Facebook will reveal that parents are particularly gushing about the specialness of their children. When I asked the parents in the group if they would feel comfortable taking a megaphone and announcing to the group how amazing and gifted their children are, most laughed at the idea and said that it was ridiculous—no one would feel comfortable doing that. And yet, this is what moms and dads all over the world are doing on social media every day, showing and telling the world how incredibly amazing little Joe is. This led to an animated discussion where a couple of moms said that, in fact, they used Facebook solely to share status updates and milestones about their children because this is what their peers appeared to be doing. If we don't do it, they suggested, others may think that our children are less special!

Surveys in the UK also confirm that almost 70 per cent of young moms use Facebook exclusively to share about their children, like a kind of online, easily accessible digital baby book. The most frequent activity of these young parents (53 per cent) was sharing or bragging about their children's achievements.[21] The strange thing was that a couple of parents said that they find it annoying when other parents go 'overboard' and gush about their child, but did not find it inconsistent that they themselves are guilty of the same behaviour.

Many parents are unaware that posting pictures of their children online has significant security concerns. Identity theft is already a major issue in many jurisdictions and posting pictures and information about your children, including which school or college they attend or graduated from, makes it that much easier for a would-be identity thief to steal their identity. A report from *Japan News* in 2013[22] detailed many instances when people were duped into submitting private information because the post seemed to be coming from friends. It appears that while people are on Facebook, they are relaxed and with their guard down, they assume that they are amongst friends. In the UK currently, 82 per cent of all identity fraud happens on the web.[23]

Frank Abagnale, the ex-conman who is depicted in the movie *Catch Me If You Can*, claims (in an interview with the *Guardian*, 2013)[24] that in the old days, he had to do a lot of research to steal identities. He would have to get information from all sorts of agencies and go through piles of material before he could build a profile of someone. Now, all he needs is to go on Facebook and if you had shared your date of birth and where you were born, he is 98 per cent on his way to steal your identity. That is how easy it is. As adults, we can say we have informed consent and are doing it to ourselves, but our children have no way of consenting when they are so young. He claims that a potential con artist can build up a complete profile of someone using Facebook simply by accessing their date and place of birth, and what they have liked or commented on. He can build a profile which will include their likes, dislikes, political and sexual orientation, among other information. Add to that an individual passport like a profile picture and you can guess how easy it is for someone to use this information if they wanted to.[25] With so many millions of children and adolescents with social media accounts, it pays for identity thieves to put a lot of effort into hacking accounts and stealing information. As parents, we ought to put in some effort to make it harder for them to access our children's information.

Secondly, as mentioned before, once we post a picture online, we give up control of it and have no idea where it might end up, so we need to do it mindfully. Recently, I came across headlines in a British newspaper about pictures of children in prom dresses and scanty clothes stolen from public Facebook profiles and Twitter feeds and being put up on a Russian website used by paedophiles.[26] The newspaper reported that the comments on these pictures from around the world made it clear that these pictures were being used by paedophiles. The proud parents and grandparents of the children had no idea that these pictures had been stolen.

Moreover, given that companies are building target customer profiles through online information gathering,[27] you can begin to appreciate how potentially risky it is to share so much information on SNSs. The Facebook environment is designed to tempt you to part with your privacy, its goal being to gather as much information from you as possible to sell targeted ads. Anyone can test this: do a couple of Google searches on something, say weight loss tips. After this, every website you open will be relentless in its pursuit of getting you to click on the link: how to lose belly fat fast. Adults theoretically have a more well-developed sense of self-control, but eventually, most adults will capitulate and click on the ad. I wonder how long it would take children? Alice Marwick, who lectures on social media and digital culture at Fordham University in New York, says that it is not difficult to imagine a future where everyone, from educational institutions to employers and banks, will consider your consumer profile (gleaned and built through what you and what others share about you) before making any major decision about you. The information that you are now posting online about your child will be the 'breadcrumb trail' that they will use to build that profile.[28]

Action points for parents

- ❏ Do a time audit for yourself to see how much time you are spending online.
- ❏ Be firm about unplugging from your devices when the family is around.
- ❏ Share with your children how you are taking your own issues with technology seriously.
- ❏ Check out the family media plan and start implementing it for yourself even before you bring it up in the family meeting.
- ❏ Be disciplined about starting and ending work. Work when you are working and switch off devices

when you are home. Customers, bosses and clients alike will respect the message that your family is important to you and you are always available for people who depend on you.

❏ Develop and stick to simple daily rituals where you will be available, for example, when making breakfast, sitting down for an after dinner coffee, reading at bedtime. Children need to know that there are tech-free times in your day when they can chat or hang out with you, free from the buzzing of incoming messages.

❏ Get to know security settings on your social media profiles and renew your knowledge, as they change frequently. Your profile and pictures are public by default. Change this setting so that the pictures are seen only by those who genuinely care about your children and want to be a part of their lives.

❏ Disable the geotagging feature on your phone which automatically records and shares the location where your picture was taken. Do not share details of birthdays or the address of your children.

❏ Consider using a pet name for your children, known only to family and friends, for posting pictures.

❏ Do not post pictures which may embarrass or compromise them in the future.

❏ As your children get older, respect their wishes about whether they are okay with the pictures and comments that you share about them.

❏ Consider sharing milestones and achievements only with close friends and family rather than posting to a wider timeline audience.

Chapter 10

Step 2: Build a Relationship with Your Children

What can you do to promote world peace?
Go home and love your family.
—Mother Teresa

Parents who were raised before the Internet age lived in an adult-centred world. Parents were in charge and everyone in the family knew it. Children were often encouraged to be seen and not heard. Although many parents did a good job in teaching their children obedience, to respect authority and other values, they often did it in an authoritarian way. Perhaps reacting to the authoritarian upbringing, the current generation of parents has swung the other way.[1] They want to befriend their children and be child-centred, moulding their lives around the children's needs. When parents are asked what they desire most for their children, many respond that it is to see their children happy. However, research shows that our lenient parenting practices have not resulted in a generation of children who are happy and well-adjusted, with enough life skills to be successful.[2]

There is, I believe, a middle path for parents, between being authoritarian and focusing only on rules and being permissive and focusing only on their children's emotional well-being. That middle path is to have a close, respectful relationship with children *and* to expect high standards of behaviour. Only when we do both can we train them in life skills and help them develop strong characters, which will set them up for mental health and success.

In this day and age, parents are often confused about what it means to have a great relationship with their children. Many parents believe that they need to be friends with their children in order to be close and communicate. This is not true. Children have their peers as friends, to have fun with, to talk and play together. Our primary job is to parent them, to keep them safe, to build their physical and emotional health and to nurture life skills and character strengths that will help them develop into confident individuals with a great relationship with themselves, others, their faith, the community and world at large. This means that parents may need to make decisions and choices that are difficult for them in the short run. As parents, it is our duty to refuse children that fourth piece of candy, because we know it will cause them harm in the long run.

In our quest to improve our relationship with our children, we can turn technology into an ally, up to a point. There is some encouraging emerging research which suggests that if we use technology as a means to get an insight into our children's world, if we use it with them in shared family activities and if we extract life lessons from its use in a sensitive and thoughtful manner, we can overcome the great divide of technology.[3]

Your ultimate leverage with children is through your relationship with them, so focus on this. Research shows that a major factor that stops children from wrongdoing is the fear of disappointing parents, so parents have a very strong role to play in modelling values.[4] We are much more powerful than we realize.

So how do we go about building a close, respectful relationship with children while still being their parent?

Building a relationship based on trust and love starts as soon as a child is born. When we respond to a baby's cries, giving her love and positive attention, it means not only building our relationship but teaching the child to trust others and to have a positive outlook on life.[5] The attachment bond formed during the first few years of life sets the tone for the parent–child relationship.[6] Although a bulk of the attachment research focuses on mothers, research has shown, for example, that dads who take time off from work to bond with their babies tend to have a closer relationship with that child for the rest of her childhood and beyond. The research suggests that this closeness is bi-directional in the sense that both parent and child initiate it.[7]

What the newborn child needs most from us is time and focused positive attention. We can spend lots of time and effort in buying our children nice things, including gadgets and so-called intelligence-building toys, but none of them can replace what we can give them through our simple presence.

Rituals of connection

As children grow, giving time and attention can strengthen and maintain the relationship. Small daily rituals can help both parent and child check in with each other and sustain the connection. In families, mornings and evenings tend to be busy and chaotic. A simple but effective practice is to mark the entrance to or exit from the home with hellos and goodbyes and be emotionally present during them. Checking in and connecting with the child before they leave home will likely give them a positive mood throughout the day. This can be as simple as getting down to the child's level, looking her in the eye, giving her a hug and saying goodbye. Similarly, when a child is welcomed home by a simple greeting by the parent, the child associates home as a relaxed, pleasant and welcoming place to be.

Bedtime rituals are also important. Children and young adults who end up in therapy often remember the times when, as children, they cried themselves to sleep and no one knew. On the other hand, others remember with fondness the daily rituals of bedtime which involved snuggling into bed with a parent or grandparent and a storybook. Daily investments of time like this will pay rich dividends in the future.

Other effective rituals are eating together on a regular basis. There is much research to confirm that eating together as a family is one of the best ways to connect with children.[8] The studies suggest that children who eat with their families are more likely to eat healthy food, have fewer issues with their body image, are less likely to be depressed, delinquent or experiment with risky or immoral behaviour, and also tend to have greater levels of academic achievements and psychological well-being.[9] What is more difficult to measure, perhaps, is the feelings of closeness, comfort and stability experienced by the family as a whole in terms of improved relationships.

Of course, in order to yield the greatest benefits, we need to be decisive about rituals. If we can encourage all or the majority of family members to be present at meals, if we eat together at least three days a week, we will have the best results.[10] If parents go all out to make mealtimes a pleasant experience, children are more likely to want to participate.

It is a good idea to make the dinner table a 'safe zone' for children by adopting a 'no-nagging' policy at dinnertime. Often, when the family gathers at the dinner table the first time in the day and everyone is in the same place, it is easy to turn mealtime into a platform for dealing with housekeeping and other issues, to delegate chores, and to follow up with a bit of nagging. While this is tempting, much will be gained if we resist the urge to do so. Mealtimes should be part of the 'sacred space' and 'sacred time' that are not only technology-free (more on that in the next chapter) but also 'nagging-free' zones. If members of the household know that they are not going to be told off at the dining table, they associate mealtimes and the dining table with pleasant conversation and family bonding and are much more likely to relax and engage in conversation with each other.

Be trustworthy

The foundation of any strong relationship is trust. When children can count on us because we have demonstrated trustworthiness, they know home is a safe haven in a chaotic world, and are more likely to turn to us in times of stress and trouble than look elsewhere.

So how can parents demonstrate trustworthiness to their children?

1. Tell them the truth. Display integrity in your daily interactions. Do not snoop on children unless you believe they are in imminent danger. If you are going to check up on them, tell them beforehand. It is much better if they moderate their behaviour beforehand rather than 'get caught redhanded'.

2. Keep your promises. There are few things more damaging to a relationship than being repeatedly let down. If you said that you would play with them at a certain time, take them out or give them a treat, do your best to stick to your commitment.

3. Show loyalty to those who are absent. If we gossip about those who are absent, especially family members, we are harder to trust.

4. Extend trust. As children grow, the amount of trust we place in them needs to grow as well. If we allow them to make mistakes and learn from them, it will build self-confidence as well as help them to recognize trust.

5. Demonstrate respect. Start by asking yourself if the way

you talk to your child or react to her would change if someone you really looked up to was watching. That is the standard that we need to adopt in our daily interactions. When we treat the child with respect, she internalizes a feeling of self-worth and associates us with feeling good about herself. She also has a standard for healthy interactions and can set boundaries for herself. Moreover, she will learn to treat others with respect.

6. Apologize and take responsibility. As parents, it is pretty much guaranteed that we will make mistakes. Resist the urge to deflect blame or become defensive and instead make a clean apology—this means that you accept and take responsibility. A trust-building apology is a very powerful message of accountability and does not mean that you condone rudeness or not following rules.

Be clear about expectations

Parents often face problems at home because no one is clear about what the rules or expectations are. While coaching families who have issues with managing children's behaviour, one of the first questions I ask is, 'What is the rule for that?' It is surprising how many families do not have clear guidelines and expectations for technology use, for example.

When we have clear guidelines for important issues like technology, it is easier to get people on the same page and to follow through with consequences. In their absence, we will often find ourselves arguing and bewildered about how to set boundaries.

Discipline wisely when dealing with less-than-desirable behaviour

Children will make mistakes. But when they do, it is an opportunity to build trust, strengthen our relationship with them and use it as a teaching moment. But all of this takes some effort on our part.

Our job is to love children, train and guide them to learning from their mistakes. In order to do this, however, we need to first manage and regulate ourselves. We cannot be in charge of our families if we cannot regulate ourselves. The skill of self-regulation is most challenged when our children go against our deepest sense of values and beliefs and what we think we have taught them. This is where all our buttons are pushed and all sorts of anxieties come to the surface.

When we are confronted with the possibility that our 'little angels' are not so little or angelic after all, a lot of stuff is triggered within us. We generally react in one of three ways:

1) We may play 'ostrich': just as an ostrich can bury its head in the sand and not pay attention to what is happening around it, parents react the same way when confronted with grim realities.

I remember my son's experience of being exposed to pornography in middle school. It was tough to confront the reality and to decide what to do about it. The email that had come to my son had also been sent to all other members of his sixth grade class. I considered what I would like in this situation: would I want to know what was going on or would I prefer to live in the utopian belief that elite and academic schools in nice neighbourhoods do not have such issues and that these children were much too young to be engaging in such behaviour? I decided that I would want to know because if I truly wanted to protect my child, I could not do so without a realistic idea of the issue I was facing and its extent.

So I decided to call the other parents in the class to inform them of what was going on. The various reactions of the parents were quite enlightening, giving me an idea of how parents feel when confronted with the same issue.

Some parents flat-out refused to believe that their child was involved. 'Not my child,' one of them said. 'He would never engage in such things.' I tried to explain that firstly, her child was not the perpetrator but the receiver and getting the email could have impacted him. She refused to believe me. It was her child who refused to share what had happened at school and I wonder whether it was simply to protect his mother who was clearly too fragile to cope with the real world.

2) We play 'tiger': when our emotions are triggered by the reality of what our child has done, we may have a 'freak-out' in the sense that we go nuts and get angry at our children or we blame others and overreact. We may tell ourselves that our intention is to 'teach them a lesson' but we do need to ask ourselves what lesson that might be.

Freak-outs inevitably result in children becoming much more secretive and stop sharing sensitive information with us. Freak-outs seldom teach them not to engage in risky behaviour. Most often, they teach kids that parents cannot handle tough news, especially about a child's mistakes or failures.

All the above results are unfortunate because they do nothing to prevent the child from making the same mistake again. Studies show that if children are allowed to discuss difficult issues at home, it greatly *decreases* their chances of engaging in risky behaviour outside the home. Therefore, it is essential to learn to manage our own freak-outs so that they do not adversely impact our children.

Judging other children harshly has the same effect—if we come down very hard on children who have made mistakes, our own children are less likely to come to us when in trouble.

3) We play 'dead duck'. When faced with imminent death, certain species of duck will play dead. It's called tonic immobility, and scientists think that the response is a defence mechanism. As parents, we resign ourselves to the fact that 'kids will be kids'. Not freaking out does not mean that we do not take action when our children lose track. It means that instead of reacting at once, we pause to take stock of the situation, calm ourselves down and then respond in a way that is helpful to the child's learning and growth.

Evidence shows that children live up to our expectations of them.[11] This means that if we expect children to go off track, teens to rebel or children to be disrespectful, that is what will happen. It is important that we have high expectations of children, *but* accept that they may not always live up to our standards. We have to be willing to put in the time and effort to train and guide them.

It is at times like these, however, that self-regulation and the management of self are most needed. Our children will learn a great deal from how we react to their misadventures and rebellions, small and big. There are two skills which are absolutely vital to managing oneself in moments like these: bite your tongue and breathe!

Biting our tongues and breathing are two essential parenting practices that we need to master. The sooner the better. Children are always trying to read our reaction to what they do. Our reaction to their misbehaviour will teach them a lot, such as whether or not to come to us if they do something wrong. To be an approachable parent in the digital age takes a lot of skill and training for us parents but it is essential.

Biting our tongue means that we do not say the first thing that comes to our mind when we are emotionally hijacked by a difficult situation. It will give us space to breathe, to get centred and then speak from a more enlightened place, using our own self-awareness and conscience to guide us.

This does not mean that we do not speak up for our values. In fact, it is essential for children to hear us speaking about our values, as they are getting value-laden messages from technology and media all the time. If we are silent, our voice will be the only one absent from the picture.

It does mean, however, that we use lecturing and sermons with great discretion and in small measure, because our words will have much more power if used judiciously. That means taking a deep breath and waiting for negative emotions to subside.

Look at the big picture

In the thick of everyday issues and daily living, it is very easy for parents to get lost in day-to-day challenges and conflicts. A key task for parents is to be patient in the moment but also to recognize the situation for what it is without blowing it out of proportion. At the end of the day, our relationship with our children is the biggest leverage we have with them. How we behave when they are being charming or how we deal with them when they are being challenging will determine the quality of our connection with them. Long after they have outgrown the nest and flown, it is their relationship with us that will have the greatest influence on them and how they choose to relate to us.

This is something it will do us well to remember!

Chapter 11

Step 3: Get to Know Your Children's World

The real danger is not that computers will begin to think like men,
but that men will begin to think like computers.
—Sydney J. Harris

Dialogue and conversation: have tech talks

We were discussing social media and specifically Facebook at a group meeting when a mother chimed in, 'I don't approve of this online socializing at all. Social media is a waste of time and I don't believe in it. I don't have a Facebook account and I don't intend to have one.' She is not the only parent who thinks like this. Some parents are rather proud of the fact that they do not follow popular culture and can be proudly counter-cultural. They happily announce the fact that they do not understand the online world, cannot see the attraction in it and have no intention of joining it. Although such an outlook might work for some parents, I do not generally recommend it as a parenting practice. Since so much of the Net Generation's world is online, if we obstinately stay away from it, refuse to get to know it or to understand its attraction, we cannot connect with the Net Generation. There will be a large and widening generational gap. So, it is essential that we visit their world to get a sense of it.

Other parents mention how they want to 'friend' their children on social media sites such as Facebook, but the children do not allow it.

Natasha, another mother, said, 'Well, we discussed the phone plan before my children, eleven and thirteen, got their cell phones. We told them that they had to be responsible in using them, that if they went over the allotted minutes, they would need to pay for them.' Natasha's talk, like in many families, centred on the economics of the phone and the plan. While it is a good start, it does not go far enough in clarifying expectations and guidelines for use.

Getting to know and understand the virtual world your children play and socialize in is very important. The second part of this book attempted to arm you with information about potential dangers. While based on research and statistics, the information presented there does not address the particular way your child is accessing and using the Internet. That is why you need to get to know their unique Internet profile. Firstly, it gives you a way to connect to your child. If you are on Facebook, you can discuss what's happening on that platform, discuss the appropriateness of the posts and use them as teaching moments. Being on the same social media platform gives you vital fodder for conversations to connect with your children.

Secondly, you can keep a virtual eye on your child. Just as you would not let your child go on play dates or sleepovers without knowing something about the family and where they live, you cannot let your child roam free and unsupervised in the virtual world. Many parents are concerned about 'snooping' on their children online because they believe it violates their children's right to privacy. But keeping an eye on your children's virtual world is not about violating privacy. It is about understanding their world and chaperoning them, if need be, to ensure their safety. By talking to your children and learning what comprises their online experience, you are building a relationship of understanding and trust with your child which will make 'snooping' much less necessary.

Talking to them about technology and participating in their online world also gives parents an insight into the thinking and development of the child. While we need to control the virtual environment of children when they are very young, this is not a sustainable option for most families as the children grow. They will become increasingly tech-savvy and have access to the Internet from anywhere when they are away from their parents' watchful eyes. If we have continued talking to them, learning from them and participating with them in online activities, we are likely to be much better informed about what their level of ethical and moral development is, and how able they are to exert self-control and make responsible choices when faced with danger online.

Thirdly, it gives you a first-hand experience of what their world is like. One of the main principles of building relationships through communication is that before you can influence others, you need to understand them. Lastly, being on the same virtual platform as your children gives you some sense of the culture there and the dangers that might be lurking. Mind you, though, this is getting harder. As more adults are getting Facebook accounts, it seems to be losing some of its attraction for teenagers, who are migrating to other social media platforms that are not yet understood or frequented by most adults. Still, given that many platforms such as Instagram, Twitter and YouTube link to Facebook, you can still get an idea of what goes on there.

The tech talk

It is important to have an ongoing dialogue with your children about their technology use. The purpose of this dialogue is multifold—just as we would have the 'sex talk' with children, to caution them, to educate them and to express our values, the 'tech talk' serves to caution children and to proactively inform them of risks they may encounter. It is true that children may be ahead of us in navigating technology and may surpass our know-how at a very early age. This sometimes stops many parents from addressing this issue. It is important to remember, however, that their assessment of risk, foresight of consequences and their self-control will very likely not develop as fast as their ability to navigate the web. For this reason, parents still have a very vital role in guiding their children's relationship to technology. This includes what they are doing online, how they are behaving, and what their high points and concerns are. The process of dialoguing makes your interaction much more meaningful. A child who has had a parent talk about the dangers of online chat groups, or has visited an online chat group in the presence of a parent, is less likely to engage in risky behaviour while online. The process of navigating the web with them and participating in their online life will have the effect of informing them of appropriate behaviour online and in preparing them to address issues of safety and appropriate use.

There are a few things to remember when we are beginning to participate in their online world, first through dialogue and then through participation.

Choose a good time to talk. Sometimes, families only discuss issues of technology use when they are trying to get a child or teen off the computer or if they have discovered something worrying. These are generally not good times to have a tech talk because everyone involved is feeling reactive. It is much more effective to set up a specific time to talk about technology, free from the trigger of a recent conflict.

Also, it is effective to have regular short conversations rather than one long marathon session. Children and young adults respond more to short, frequent booster sessions. Parents also need to remember that there are new dangers online every day and there is no room for complacency. If we have participated online with them learning about the dangers, how to protect themselves and how and who to report it to, it will likely get imbedded somewhere in their minds so they can figure out what to do in a difficult situation. They will know they can take a parent, teacher or other trusted adult into confidence.

As the questions below suggest, it is more effective to engage the child in dialogue and conversation, which means that you will be asking as many questions as making suggestions and expressing values. The more time you spend understanding their online experience and what makes it valuable for them, the more likely you are to have an impact through your words and statements.

Great times to have value-based talks are during meals, at bedtime and in the car. You can use the questions to get started below. They are not intended to be used as a torturous interview! They are there to give parents some idea of points to look out for. Keep coming back to the questions to check your knowledge of your child's virtual life. It will keep changing, so it is important to keep the conversation going. It is not meant as a one-off conversation, but instead, to improve communication about technology, to signal to your child that you are available, that you are courageous enough to hear the truth, that if you don't know the answer, you will help figure it out with your child. Also, that you will not freak out if you hear something disturbing but will support your child in coming up with a workable solution for you and for the family. (A message of value that we can give children is that their behaviour has an impact on others, starting with the immediate family.)

The frame or context has to be that you are trying to understand their world because you care about them and are interested in what they care about. At the same time, share things that you find interesting online—don't be hesitant to tag them in interesting posts but use this resort cautiously. If the children think that you are covertly trying to reform them on a public platform, it will not augur well for the future of your online relationship!

Please do not use these questions as interview questions or ask them all at the same time! They are:

- ❑ What are your favourite websites and apps? What do you do enjoy about these sites? What makes these apps 'sick' (cool)?
- ❑ What websites are your friends into right now?
- ❑ Which is your favourite social media website? Can we please be friends online? What are your concerns?
- ❑ Can you show me things that you enjoy online? Funny or popular YouTube videos? Why do you think this particular video has gone viral? What makes it so interesting to your friends?
- ❑ While you are online, have you ever been contacted by someone you didn't know? When and where? Did you wonder how they found you? How did you answer? Did it make you feel uncomfortable? How can I support you in addressing this?
- ❑ Have you ever received a message on your phone that was mean, rude or disrespectful? How did you respond? Do you or your friends ever text things that are mean or hurtful?
- ❑ How do you keep yourself safe when you are on the Internet?
- ❑ Have you ever had to delete a post or comment on your page that was written by someone else? Was it embarrassing or rude? Why did you have to delete it?

- ❐ Do you use Snapchat? Please show me how it works. Do you think pictures ever really vanish? What if someone takes a screenshot?
- ❐ What kind of personal information are you posting online? Have you ever posted your full name? Age? School? Phone number? Current location?
- ❐ Can you show me how privacy settings on Facebook work? What settings do you have on currently? How often do you check and change these?
- ❐ Generally, what kind of digital dramas happen on social media sites these days? Is it a good idea for friends to vent on a public social media platform?
- ❐ Do any of your friends or others know your password for any social media site or app?
- ❐ Are you comfortable showing me blogs, posts and videos that you have published online? What kind of stuff do you post? Do you have any personal guidelines before posting?

Chapter 12

Step 4: Set Limits

We need to re-create boundaries. When you carry a digital gadget
that creates a virtual link to the office, you need to create a
virtual boundary that didn't exist before.
—Daniel Goleman

Setting limits and boundaries is a vital part of our job as parents. Rules and limits give a sense of security to the child because they know what is expected of them. They also provide a sense of order in the household by allowing everyone to be on the same page. Once we have a relationship with our children and know the realities that operate in their world, we can set about making rules and limitations on their Internet use.

Having said that, parents are sometimes concerned about the conflicting information or advice they read on the Internet, and this often seems to get a pushback from children. Once we accept, however, that it is unrealistic to expect enthusiasm from children about limits to their freedom, and that we have to raise healthy, well-functioning children who will be an asset to our family and the world, we will be more confident about setting limits. If our children are to be responsible human beings in a constantly plugged-in world, if they are to learn to coexist with technology but not let it rule them, then the limits will have to be set by us. Neither their peers nor the present-day culture is going to do it.

It appears, in fact, that people who are most entrenched in the world of technology appear to set the strictest limitations on their children. Steve Jobs, the late founder of Apple Computers, is a case in point. When Nick Bilton from the *New York Times* interviewed him in 2010, Jobs said, 'They haven't used it (the iPad). We limit how much technology our kids use at home.'[1] Chris Anderson, the CEO of 3D Robotics, has such stringent rules in his household for his five children that his children accuse his wife and him of 'being fascists'. He said that his kids complain that he and his wife are 'overly concerned about tech, and they say that none of their friends have the same rules...That's because we have seen the dangers of technology first-hand. I've seen it in myself, I don't want to see that happen to my kids.'[2]

In light of what tech-savvy parents do, it is worrying that the majority of parents do not set any limits. In a study involving both children and parents, 46 per cent of parents said that they set some limits, while only 36 per cent of the children said that their parents set rules for Internet use.[3] The discrepancy in results could be due to the fact that in this study, half the children had computers in their rooms.[4] With computers in the rooms, it is very likely that rules, even if they exist, would very likely go out of the window. If children have access to the mobile Internet in the shape of cell phones and tablets, setting and enforcing rules is even more problematic. So it is essential to realize it is not a good idea to have unlimited Internet access for anyone in the house. Without limits, being online can easily become the default mode.

I do believe that tech-centric families can do as well as tech-light families in terms of family strength and children's well-being if they are decisive about their tech habits. As a general rule of thumb, it is a good idea to allocate proportionate online time with offline time. Dr Larry Rosen, an expert psychologist in this field, recommends that for very young children, between 70 to 80 per cent of their free time should ideally be tech-free.[5] So, for example, if they have spent twenty minutes watching a

YouTube video or playing with a child-friendly app, they need to spend between an hour and a half to two hours in non-tech-related activities such as colouring, playing, reading, building blocks and so on. For older children, the time allowed to stay online will gradually grow and young teens can be allowed up to an hour at a time, while for older teens, the maximum time allowed in front of a screen should be two hours at a stretch. After this, Dr Rosen explains that it is vital that the brain's neural pathways reset and engage in non-tech-related activities, such as face-to-face connection to other human beings, and to encourage imagination and creativity.[6]

Create sacred space in your home and sacred time in your day

Sacred space means creating tech-free places in your home where there is no Internet or phone. Creating a tech-free space ensures that family members get used to the idea that technology must be used in its proper place, available but not something the family becomes so dependent on that it overtakes every aspect of family life and time.

If we can maintain a boundary between work and home, between attention to those who are remote to those who are immediately around us and craving our attention, we will have already gone a long way in managing technology in our family life. It is crucial that your children feel your commitment and attention several times a day without distraction. Ideally, the sacred space should be the eating and sleeping areas of the house, although in the plugged-in society of today, this is easier said than done.

When the children are young, it is up to the parents to establish the sanctity of the bedroom. Many couples comment that a decision not to have a television or telephone in their bedrooms contributed to the health of their marriage. When you are in a child's bedroom reading to them or putting them to bed, leave your phone behind so you give your child undivided attention. Time spent before bed is a wonderful opportunity to connect with children as we wind down the day. It is a precious time to share stories and create memories that will be downloaded into their emotional hard drive, so to speak.

In any case, the radiation from technological devices, as we know, has been known to interfere with sleep cycles and the amount of deep sleep we get. Children are especially vulnerable to this for they need more sleep as they are growing.

Bushra, a woman in her thirties, struggles to maintain the sanctity of mealtimes. She says, 'During dinner conversation, even if we are talking about something interesting, my husband Bashir will pull out his phone to check the facts on Google. If we are making plans to go out for a meal or to visit, he will immediately pull out his calendar to see if he is free. I feel like we are never alone. There is always something vying for his attention. I feel ridiculous that I am jealous of his phone, but I am!'

Amit expresses a similar frustration. 'With my wife, mealtimes are like a never-ending business meeting, with her adding tasks onto her "to do" list, putting things on the calendar and sending a quick email about something we are discussing. I would like to have an old-fashioned family conversation without Mr Google and Mr Google Calendar being a part of it.'

Family dinnertime

It is worth devoting special attention to dinnertime. We talked about the research on the benefits of family dinnertime in the last chapter, and mentioned that there is much research to suggest that it is a special opportunity every day to strengthen family bonds and inoculate children against the toxins of pop culture and environment.

With so many benefits, it is a no-brainer that we should invest time and energy in this family ritual so that we can reap some of the benefits. Of course, we need to follow some basic guidelines to make the most of the ritual.

Needless to say, it needs to be a technology-free time and zone. Sita and Mithul shared how they have put a pretty basket at the entrance to the kitchen so that it is a visual reminder that everyone needs to put their phones in before coming to the dining table. At the beginning, Sita says, it was challenging. 'I had to post a sign above the basket "Switch off your phones" and "Entering a tech-free zone" to remind everyone to do this. The basket was right outside the kitchen and people would often "forget" to silence the phone, so the pings and rings could be heard inside the kitchen while we were eating, taking our attention momentarily away from our conversation.' Sita and Mithul persevered, however, and found that it became easier and more automatic with time. The children began to look forward to the tech-free meal (although they still murmured discontent about it, from time to time).

This shows that with some perseverance, we can actually lessen our continued dependence on our devices. Here are a few recommendations for families to remember to create tech-free zones in their home.

1. It is best to have central docking and charging stations for family devices so that everyone can 'turn in' their devices at certain times.
2. It is best not to have the docking and charging stations for technology in the kitchen or in the bedroom. If at all possible, the stations should be outside the kitchen and bedroom, otherwise it is much too tempting to plug the

phone into the charger and then 'forget' to switch it off. If we are not strict with such rules, it will be extremely challenging to follow them.

3. There will be times when children will want to take photos of the food because that is what young people do these days. If you want to consider allowing this, you can ask them to take pictures before everyone sits down and then leave the phone outside the kitchen.

Now if family members are making the sacrifice to come to the table without their phones, we need to ensure that we make it worthwhile by following some basic rules:

1) No lecturing, even about technology. If our intention is to build connection and trust, we need to manage our impulse to lecture them or tell them off while we have their attention. Children will quickly get on board if they can trust that dinnertime is truly sacred—also as a lecture-free zone.

2) Conflict-free zone. Even if people are at each other's throats during the day, the evening meal should be a time when they can (even temporarily) let go of their hurt and resentments and focus on the harmonious parts of being a family.

3) Time to catch up and reconnect. Creating a sacred time and space in your home can be likened to unplugging from our devices but plugging into the source of happiness and fulfilment that a family can give us—it nourishes our hearts and our souls.

If we follow these simple steps, we can ensure that we can provide:

1) Predictability: training ourselves and our families that some factors are too important and sacred to be overtaken by

technology. It gives children a lot of security when they can count on something in the family that happens at a predictable, set time.

2) Connection: that even if during the day we are too busy running around and being immersed in devices, we can maintain real-life connections with our family members without the mediation of technology.

3) Communication at the table: if we are not talking about conflict, we can actually focus on building communication with our family members. We can begin by asking them about the high and low points of their day, what their dreams and aspirations are, or talking about news and other stories and using those as teaching moments to discuss and clarify values. If we build this kind of communication routine in the home, our children will learn vital relationship skills, which will serve them well, even in a high-tech lifestyle.

Have longer connection rituals on a weekly and yearly basis

When we set aside half a day or an evening to reconnect as a family, it strengthens bonds. While daily rituals of connection are vital, during weekdays they may often become short and sometimes hurried. An afternoon or an evening set aside just for family fun can 'top up' the connection ritual. Families who set aside a specific night of the week for a game night, for example, often remark that it fosters better communication during the rest of the week, and family members appear to get along better. Playing games together also teach children important life skills, such as how to lose gracefully. Many young adults and parents have remarked that pleasant memories from their childhood frequently surfaced when the family was gathered together having fun. Ideally, of course, the game night should be non-tech-related, although some families do very well with playing video or Wii games together. If you are using tech games on a family night, it may be a good idea to alternate from week to week from tech games to those that are non-tech-based.

Many families find that despite their best efforts, they go off track from time to time and tech slowly creeps up in their life to overtake family time. At times like this, it is a good idea to do a 'digital detox'. Like a health detox, a digital detox resets the brain's addiction to technology so that the family can get back on track to what is a desirable relationship with technology. A proactive and conscious mother of four young children, Marina says, 'We always use our family vacations to detox digitally. Being away from home and having fun timings scheduled makes it easier. While we are away on vacation, we do not pay for roaming data, which automatically cuts phone use by a large amount. Initially, the children tend to huddle outside coffee shops and restaurants looking for free Wi-Fi, but that usually wears off in the first twenty-four hours as we get into the spirit of the holiday. We sometimes consciously leave our phones in the hotel room to make it easier, and have invested in a digital camera to take pictures with instead of using our phones.'

Marina's family is fortunate to be able to take trips to detox but it is not necessary to go away in order to accomplish this. Just like a healthy diet, a digital detox involves setting an intention, having a plan, and taking action in order to achieve it. It is helpful to start with three days and build it up to a week when you only engage with technology very minimally. It is also very effective to make it into a game with challenges and possibly (non-tech!) prizes so that children of all ages can participate enthusiastically.

Dealing with others in our home

An issue that parents frequently mention is when the children's friends or other family members visit your place but do not have the same rules about technology. When you have family over, it can be hard to control phone use by other people. Shai, a mom in the parent group, took some drastic measures and installed signal blockers in parts of her house. Many other parents thought that this idea was pure genius because it takes away so much monitoring and nagging.

Not every family will want to go that route. Other families have used humour with good results. Lamya Patel says she spends a lot of time preparing gourmet meals for guests and would rather they enjoy the food without being distracted by their phone. She keeps a basket on the front table and jokes with guests as they walk in, 'The special for tonight is incompatible with your phone, so please place it in this basket.' She said that after a few times, people realized that they had survived the night without gadgets and quite enjoyed it. She said that many friends remarked that evenings at the Patels' house are always full of great conversation and they now expect it to be a no-phone zone.

Pictures

It sometimes appears that in the twenty-first century, reporting and documenting our lives has become more important than living it. Whether it is at a family dinner, a wedding or a family holiday, people are busy sharing the moment with those who are not there rather than being present for those who are. It is almost like saying outright, 'Other people out there, who are not present, are more important than you are.' Although posting pictures can allow family members who could not make it to the event, for example, feel part of the celebrations, it is almost as if the experience is simply an excuse to post about it. Given how common it has become and how tempting it is for children and adults to post without thinking, it may be a good idea to consider setting limits on taking and posting of pictures.

The Patels also have a sensible policy for taking and posting pictures. At any event or celebration or restaurant they go to, they will announce, 'Picture time!' Everyone takes out their phone and shoots pictures for a set amount of time. Then, they put away their cameras for the rest of the event. They always wait until they get home to post the pictures on social media if they decide they want to share the pictures. Amit adds, 'The people present at the event should see a lot more of your face without a camera or a smartphone in front of it.' Lamya did say that it is not an ideal situation and they 'miss many good Instagram-worthy shots'. 'What we gain, though, is far more valuable,' she notes. 'Being present and engaged in the event without technology pulling our attention away helps us remember the event and the people that made it special in a very real way. If we spend the time taking pictures, we will have the pictures but accompanying it will be an empty feeling because we did not actually connect with anyone while we were there. Nor did we experience the event with all our senses and attention.'

Family agreements on tech use

Many families draw up formal contracts for tech use, which can be very effective in getting everyone on the same page about what the expectations and rules are for technology use in the home. In the absence of contracts and limits, arguments and conflicts about tech use will arise and a resolution difficult to reach since everyone ends up arguing from different world-views.

Do not expect enthusiasm or endorsement of agreements at

the beginning. The older the children are, the more likely they are to resist. Remember that not every decision we make as parents is going to be popular in the short run. You do your job and let them do what they will. Having said that, there are some steps that you can take to minimize a pushback from the rest of the family.

1. Call a family meeting to discuss family tech-use. It is much more effective to discuss such a potentially hot topic away from the triggers of conflict. In fact, an ideal time to have a meeting is before upgrading to the next new gadget. It is much easier to plan and set rules ahead of time rather than reactively, when the new piece of technology is already causing problems in the family. Pick a time when everyone is in a pleasant mood and more likely to be open to parental influence. After a good meal is sometimes the best time!

2. Begin by saying something along the lines of:
   'I am concerned that our unlimited tech-use is causing us to lose touch with each other. Family time and being present for one another is very important to me, and I want to make sure that we create time and place for our family when we can be together without technology, so that we can focus on each other instead of on our phones. So let's talk about some rules that we can all live with.'

   Notice that in these words, the parent is taking responsibility for how he or she feels about technology use. There is no blaming the children, but is framed as a family issue voicing the parent's awareness that the rules need to be fair to both children and parents.

3. Brainstorm rules. It is very helpful to involve the whole family in this and parents are often surprised when children come up with more stringent rules than the parents

themselves! During brainstorming, welcome all ideas and do not evaluate them until everyone has had a chance to express what their ideal contract would look like.

4. Brainstorm about consequences. Ask all family members to come up with possible consequences of not adhering to the contract. Doing this as a group exercise will lead to a lot of creativity. It also avoids the common parent trap of taking away all access to technology for a certain period of time. Many parents react in a moment of anger and set unsustainable consequences for a breach of the rules. We need to strike a balance since access to technology is the average Net Gen's lifeline—not only does it appear unfair, the parent does not have too much leverage when there is actually serious misbehaviour.

   The stronger your relationship is with your child, the firmer you can be. It is hard to set limits when your relationship is shaky, so we need to build the relationship first, using the suggestions in the previous chapter. Of course, you may find that the process of having a meeting and discussing this issue as a family is also a strengthening experience. In case of a tie or non-agreement, parents need to retain the deciding vote or veto power for any clause in the agreement. Giving a voice to all members of the family does not mean that if children are in the majority, they can hijack the process. It means that you will hear all sides of the story, note the concerns of all family members, and in case of non-agreement, will decide using compassion and wisdom.

5. Pick rules and consequences to try for a set period. It is helpful to have a trial period for this contract. A period of two or more weeks is a good amount of time to see how it is working. It encourages everyone to commit to trying it

without feeling that they are stuck in it forever, if it does not work for them.

6. Draft up a family agreement or contract. After the contract is drafted, get one of the younger members of the family to read it out so that everyone can hear what they have agreed to, and get everyone to sign it.

7. Have a follow-up meeting after two weeks. Start by appreciating everyone for trying and talk about what worked. After this, you can discuss what could be better or what rules need to be tweaked or changed.

Keep the process of meeting and tweaking the agreements going until you settle on a regime that works for everyone. Expect that as things change and children grow, you will need to keep visiting the contract again and again.

As parents, we need to be realistic and cannot expect that things will go perfectly all the time. If you are on track 80 per cent of the time, you are doing really well. If you slip, and most families do, just keep getting back on track.

When are you likely to slip?

Research finds that the three most likely times when parents turn to technology as a parenting tool are:

1) When they are busy making dinner or working, that is, they use it as a baby sitter

2) To calm down an upset child

3) As a reward for good behaviour or as a consequence for bad behaviour

This is problematic because it links the reward systems in the brain with technology. When the child is upset, what is really needed is to give him self-soothing tools to manage and regulate his own emotions. By giving them technology at that time, we are distracting them and not giving them an opportunity to learn very valuable life skills. As parents, we really need to be okay with the fact that our children are not always going to be happy, nor is it our job to ensure that they always are. In fact, one of the main differences and hallmarks of our parenting style in this generation is that we pursue children's short-term happiness over their long-term well-being. This may be well-meaning but it does not result in happy children.

Entertaining and distracting children

Parents are human and generally have less energy than their offspring. Throughout the ages, parents have used various means to distract unhappy children and to entertain bored and edgy ones. We were given various toys, pacifiers and so on to calm us down when we were children. So, what then is the issue with giving children technology to calm and distract them, especially since it appears to work so very well?

Let us take a look at using a favourite toy as an example: a stuffed toy will calm and soothe a child because it provides familiarity and comfort. The child associates the toy with a peaceful environment; it calms the nervous system and provides a connection. Technology, on the other hand, is *not* a replacement for a favourite toy. Technology, by its nature, is stimulating, not calming. When a baby's brain (and also an adult's, for that matter) gets used to a certain level of stimulation, it forms a new benchmark for 'normal'. Just as people who use drugs need a higher and higher dose to get to and maintain the same level of high, the brain also resets the normal level and craves more and more stimulation to get the dopamine high that gives it the sense of well-being.

Also, distracting ourselves by technology is extremely easy. Once we get used to the ease, it is extremely difficult to turn to distractions that are harder to use but more valuable in our life. This is true generally in all areas of life but especially so in technology. Because it works so well, we are less likely to turn to other less engaging things to distract or entertain us.

Add to this the fact that technology does nothing to foster self-regulation and self-control skills, which children need more than ever in the age of technology. By being taught to look at external sources to entertain and engage them, they get the message very early on that the answer to all of life's questions and troubles is to log on and zone out. The ability to plod on, be persistent, wade through periods of boredom and confusion are all lost in the age of instant distraction, and yet, these are the very skills that children need to navigate the modern world and thrive mentally and emotionally.

Using technology as a reward and punishment

Insiya was very frustrated. 'I have tried everything to lessen my six-year-old's addiction to the iPad. I carefully watch and supervise everything she watches, but if she does not get her daily dose of it, she is cranky and throws tantrums until she gets what she wants. It is the best way to control her behaviour because if she is disobedient, all I have to do is to threaten to take away the iPad and she falls back into line.'

Remember to acknowledge and appreciate your family for the efforts that they are making towards making the family stronger. The more you focus on what people are doing right, the more encouraged they are and likely to feel good about themselves, the more buy-in you will get.

Just one more note of caution: many families notice that when they start putting the tech meeting and family agreement in place, things begin to improve fairly quickly and conflict lessens. It is when families become complacent about the agreements that they begin to think that they are not needed. As Sherry pointed out, 'What we did not realize was that the reason things were going so well is because we were having family meetings. We became intentional about our relationship to technology, as you suggested, and it really worked! When we let the meetings slide, we slackened following the agreements. Now, we recognize that family meetings are a protective factor in our family.'

Family tech agreements

Please use the points given here as a guide to make your own contracts. They should be talking points to be discussed at the family meeting and then decided. Your children are much more likely to adhere to the contract if they are involved in creating and signing the contract.

Once everyone has signed the agreement, it gives you an external standard to enforce and can potentially take away nagging for every infraction of time on the net. The more well-thought-out your contract is, and the more the whole family is involved in reassessing it, the easier it will be to enforce because family members will keep everyone accountable.

Setting rules and enforcing them has to be in the context of building our relationship with our children. If our relationship is close, all of this will be easy. If it is not, no amount of rule setting is going to fix the conflict in the family.

Some points:

When are family members allowed to have certain devices?

Who pays for them? Who pays for usage and who replaces them if lost or damaged?

When, where and how will they use the devices?

What is your role in monitoring?

How will you be involved in your children's virtual life?

What is the general etiquette?
What are the rules?
What are the consequences?
How stringent are the rules for privacy?

Sample contract used by the Patel family

I understand that using technology such as my smartphone or tablet is a privilege which needs to be respected. In using this privilege, I agree to the following responsibilities:

Children's Expectations

1. I will take care of my phone and keep it charged at all times.
2. I will always answer the phone when my mom or dad call. If I am at a place where cell phones are not allowed or not working, I will call back as soon as I possibly can.
3. I will respect the technology-free times and zones of this family, as outlined below.
4. I will respect the curfew times as determined by my parents.
5. I will not text, email or say anything through this device I would not say in person to my friends or to strangers.
6. I will only download apps or games after showing them to my parents. I understand that I may have to wait until the family meeting to discuss and get approval.
7. I will not take or post pictures of others without their permission.
8. I will not send pictures or messages that would make me uncomfortable if my parents or the receiver's parents see them.
9. I will keep myself updated with the privacy settings on my favourite sites and apps and discuss these with my parents.
10. My parents may decide to check on my phone to ensure

that I am following rules for my safety. I will share my password with them.

11. I will never agree to meet someone in person who I met online.
12. I will respect the cell phone use policy of public places that I go to. I will always remember to turn off my phone when visiting the temple, the hospital, the library or other quiet places.
13. I will always look at people when they are talking to me. I understand that the phone can turn my attention from people who I am with. I will be mindful of using my phone when others are around.

Parents' Expectations

1. I will not let my phone or tablet distract me when my child is trying to get my attention.
2. We will set reasonable limits on technology use after listening to all members of the family. Even though everyone will have the opportunity to be heard, it is ultimately our responsibility as parents to set rules and implement them for the good of this family.
3. I will get to know my children's digital world and try to understand it before trying to set rules.
4. I will not unnecessarily invade my child's privacy. I will only do what is essential to ensure my child's safety online.

Chapter 13

Step 5: Build a Community of Support

The power of one, if fearless and focused, is formidable,
but the power of many working together is better.
—Gloria Macapagal Arroyo

I was talking to a colleague recently who argued that, 'We do not raise our children. Our children are raised by the media, their peer, and the school system. As parent, we have very little control over how they turn out.' As I have reiterated repeatedly throughout this book, I believe that contrary to what my social worker colleague believes, parents actually have a very powerful influence on their child's life. Having said that, the environment, the peers, the school system and other factors all may greatly influence a child and how he or she turns out.

It is also true that if we have a community of support, people and organizations that echo our values, it makes our job infinitely easier and is a major protective factor for our children. In close-knit communities, counting on one another's presence and support and watching out for each other's children used to be the heart of the community in the past. Many experts believe that the weakening of community ties lies at the heart of family and social ills that exist in society today.

So, even if you are genuinely hands-on and conscious parents with children who accept and internalize your values, being part of a community of like-minded individuals is like a protective net that supports us and catches us when we fall. Raising a child is hard. Parenting by itself, even as a nuclear family, is tough work. There is no time to fall sick or take a day off. Being on call

all the time is exhausting, so when there are people to fall back on, it eases the stress on the parent just a little bit.

When children are young, parents often say that they miss the proverbial village that looks after a child because they would greatly welcome the support of an extra pair of hands or eyes to help. They remember the old quote, 'It takes a village to raise a child' and wistfully reminisce about how it was relatively easier for their own parents to raise them due to the presence of many people ready to help out.

However, the benefits provided by the village go far beyond babysitting and giving respite to exhausted parents. The presence of loving adults outside the immediate family offers positive role models for children and gives them valuable life lessons in getting along with a diversity of individuals. In many eastern cultures, including South Asian culture, there is the concept of 'like kin' where family, friends and community members are treated as if they were related.

Those who do not have access to it feel the absence of this extended family system keenly. For diaspora families who have no extended family around, it is very important to create a support system. Often, when parents start a new family, they get so caught up in the day-to-day of parenting that they are not able to reach out to others. If the support is not already present, it is hard to focus attention on it. And yet, it is important to recognize that reaching out and forming a community may take some determination and effort in the short term but will make our jobs much easier in the long run.

Moreover, although it is good to have strong values and not buy into popular culture, we also do not want to be 'weirdos', the only ones who don't talk on the phone while in restaurants or who do not take their phone into the dining room. We would like to feel a sense of belonging and shared values in at least some communities and people we interact with on a regular basis. In this chapter, let us discuss finding such a community, and if there doesn't appear to be one, building one so that we have that safety net.

Building a community

To even talk about finding or building a community is a uniquely modern predicament. In the days of hyper-connectivity, it is ironic that we need to make an effort to connect with people who are not connected via tech 24/7. In the old days, family outings meant many adults were casually present. Children tended to socialize with all generations present, with social groupings being casual, fluid and seamlessly incorporating members of different generations. Unknown to children, this interaction taught them many valuable skills including respect, talking to adults, compassion for the young and helping them, being part of a bigger family and recognizing the benefits, responsibilities and challenges that go with it—being part of the bigger whole. The issues of finding babysitting or childcare for children, a major concern of parents, specially working parents today, was not a concern as there were always plenty of reliable people to turn to.

Children today spend most of their time with peers, either online or in person. There is a significant lack of adult presence and guidance for many youth. Some of this peer-to-peer interaction was so designed by adults and has the unintended consequence of further depriving children of connections with adults. Let us take faith communities as an example. The practice of faith and attendance at worship services has traditionally been a family affair. Now, many faith communities are introducing youth programming, partly as an effort to engage youth by making religion more relevant to their lives.

Enlightened religious programming can certainly have this impact, but if it is not balanced with events that involve the whole family, it will serve to further deprive youth of adult guidance and an opportunity to receive mentoring. Adults can also provide a sense of history and share the lived experience of faith and its challenges.

With extended families spread further apart, the casual presence and intermixing of different generations has become increasingly rare, being relegated to special occasions and celebrations. Even when different generations are present, the norm of grandparents, parents, uncles, aunts and children happily cohabiting and socializing in the same physical space has significantly changed. Even when families are in the same space or children are out with adults, it is acceptable for them to 'do their own thing' or retreat into their virtual world, a world where they mostly socialize only with peers and roam unsupervised by caring adults.

It is no wonder that so many young people feel insecure and lost. In previous generations, several adults from the extended family and beyond would have intervened and demanded that the children interact with the greater family. Children would have been expected not only to be present but also to make a meaningful contribution to family events. Changing parenting norms now give considerable discretion and choice to children in all aspects of their lives, including their social lives. These are choices that the children are not necessarily ready to make.

Given the modern norm of peer-to-peer socializing, both for youth and adults, rebuilding the 'village' will not be automatic. It will need to be intentional and a team of support will have to be composed before the builders create opportunities for cross-generational mingling. The good news is that just one person can start a movement. Some suggestions on how to go about building a community, which provides support to its members and looks out for the welfare of its young, follow.

Let us firstly look at building our own team of support and then consider how we can provide tech-free community building opportunities for our children.

Building our team

As parents, you can start the process of building a team by thinking of three to six adults you would want as part of the care team for your children and your family. They may be like-minded people who care for you and your children, key individuals, such as family friends you consider as mentors, someone from the faith community, and possibly a member from your children's school community.

It is very important to include someone from the school community as school is a significant part of children's lives. Just a generation ago, teachers were so revered that parents supported them in whatever discipline they meted out to children. With the increasing focus on ensuring children's short-term happiness, often parents will side with their child if they have been been disciplined at school. This undermines teachers and puts them on the defensive. Too often today, teachers and parents find themselves in opposing corners rather than united in ensuring children's welfare. This 'divorce in the neighbourhood', as Ron Taffel calls it, has not been good for the welfare of children.[1] In order to rebuild the village, parents need to give respect back to the teachers, accept that they are on the same team, reach out to them and invite them to be on the same page. In my experience, educators tend to be more sensible about what children need because they are less emotionally involved and have seen the results of permissive parenting first hand. They are also trained to have an enlightened sense of what is good for children in the long run. In order to gather support from teachers, it is essential that we bring back respect for the teachers in our homes.

Parenting groups

Many first-time parents find parent support groups extremely helpful. The purpose of the mutual support group is to share ideas and exchange information about challenges and solutions of common parenting issues. These parenting groups can be your lifeline in providing support. A good place to find such parenting groups is through the school's Parent Teacher Association, or the local library or community centre. If there is no group running in your area, it is fairly easy to start one by finding a place to meet and advertising in local newspapers or community bulletin boards. Of course, there are many virtual groups which can be found through Facebook, but given that one of the purposes of this group would be to provide real time face-to-face interaction, it is much better to start a live in-person group.

Faith and community groups

A ready made potential source of support is your faith or community group. The temple, mosque or church already has structures built in to foster relationships and provide support. For families to reap the full benefit of support and mentorship for the family, it is important to be more involved than simply showing up for regular worship times. If the family is involved in the life of the congregation, building ties and meeting people outside the place of worship, you will get the full experience of community life. Children may likely complain about attending religious services, but if the family prioritizes attendance, the children get the message that community life is important. If you occasionally allow them to skip, the whining will likely continue and may increase. The benefits of attendance at a church or synagogue or other place of worship are not seen on a weekly basis but accrue over a period of time. So the best advice for parents is to consciously ignore their attitude.

Volunteering and community service

A great way to get involved in the life of the congregation is to volunteer as a family. Community service, such as visiting the sick or working at a soup kitchen, has multiple benefits. It allows children to mingle with people of different generations outside their social circle. It teaches them responsibility, empathy and compassion. It allows them to make a positive contribution to their community and gives them the confidence that what they do matters. Research shows that reaching out to others and making a positive contribution is correlated to happiness and is a protective factor against depression.[2] Studies show that teenagers who manage to avoid many stumbling blocks of youth today have community service in common.[3]

Aasia complained about her mother, 'When we go to family events or dinner parties with the family, I am the only loser who is not allowed to access my cell phone,' says the fifteen-year-old. 'I sit there staring at everyone's faces while they are busy messaging each other and I feel left out.'

This young lady's predicament is not unique. The downside of raising children who are mindful consumers of technology is that they will act in a counter-cultural way, and unless your child is full of self-esteem and confidence, it is going to be hard for her. So what are parents to do in a situation like that?

Let us consider a few options in handling a situation like this.

Firstly, you need to empathize with the difficulty the child faces and appreciate the effort to be mindful. When the child is complaining, it is not the time to lecture about the downside of the Internet—children already know that, which is why they can hold out when everyone else is on their phones.

Secondly, instead of your own suggestions, ask them to brainstorm ways of making the situation less challenging. Parents are usually hesitant to take this step because they imagine that children will always want to take the easiest way out and are often surprised when they manage to honour their parents' values, and at the same time, their own social circles.

This is what Aasia and her mother exchanged in the parent group, with very little help from either myself or the other parents.

Aasia: So, it is annoying and lame that everyone is on the phone when we go to Auntie Zee's house and I am just hanging out.

Nadia: Hmm, so it sounds like you feel left out of the conversation?

Aasia: Well, sort of. Because they are texting each other and I don't have my phone with me.

Nadia: Is there anything else?

Aasia: Well, I think it is lame and rude.

Nadia: Do you want to brainstorm suggestions about how you could manage this?

Aasia: Yeah, sure. Whatever.

Nadia: You could tell them how you feel.

Aasia: I could suggest that they play board games instead.

Nadia: You could take your Wii over.

Aasia: Yes! They were saying they want that too. I could play with the baby while they are on their phones.

Nadia: Would you enjoy that?

Aasia: Yes! I love him. And he is always bugging his big brother to play, but if I entertain him while his brother is busy, he may actually play with me!

Thirdly, and this takes more time, each of us can build a supportive community which will help us live our values around technology. In the parenting group, the group had the task of taking one step to bring someone else on board with managing technology. Once parents got going on this project, they found it surprisingly easy to induct other parents in their way of thinking because many people were silently struggling with these issues *or* had not given it much thought—once they heard about the dangers of the Internet, they were ready to try.

Here are some of the suggestions and tips that the parents came up with:

- ❏ Ask the school to bring a technology and parenting expert to talk to the parents at school.
- ❏ In the community centre or school, give out tip sheets.
- ❏ Encourage your local faith-based centre to address the issue of managing technology via sermons and in meetings.
- ❏ Read out passages from this book at a parenting meeting or book club.
- ❏ Look for opportunities to connect with other parents. Strike up a conversation with other parents when waiting in school for pick-up time. Leave your phone in the car!
- ❏ Wait patiently at the doctor's or optician's office. Resist the temptation to whip out your phone. Instead, practise the ancient art of small talk with those waiting with you.
- ❏ Smile at people walking past you or waiting for the elevator.
- ❏ Borrow something from the neighbour to get chatting.
- ❏ Get your children to drop off some food for a neighbour.
- ❏ Encourage your children to offer their services to elderly neighbours or those with small children.
- ❏ Revive the tradition of handwritten letters.
- ❏ Hire a neighbourhood child to help you with a chore.

Epilogue

I wrote this book as a means to awaken parents like you to the reality out there, to help you understand its impact on our families and to offer suggestions on how to navigate this new reality. The advice in this book is not meant to supersede or to interfere with your own parental instincts. I firmly believe that it is you, the parent, who knows your own child intimately. I encourage you to trust your gut and your instinct, no matter what any so-called expert, including myself, tells you. Our children will greatly benefit if we are hands-on, if we educate ourselves and yet retain confidence in our ability to do what is best for our children.

You may have noticed that this book contains suggestions and practices to implement in our families, many of which may not deal directly with technology. The book deals less with the technical aspects of controlling the hardware or software of our devices and more with controlling our own behaviour. As technology changes, it is difficult to keep track of how to manage or control it. The principles upon which a strong family is built, however, are timeless. I believe that it makes sense to focus on these and to work on our family values so that our children can thrive, regardless of the cultural and technological climate around them. An important side benefit of this approach is that its impact is far-reaching and such parenting practices influence more than just our relationship to technology.

A topic of discussion that comes up frequently in parenting discussions about technology is the question of whether or not parents should spy on their children by checking their browsing history and/or installing spy software on computers. Spy software is of many types but the most popular ones keep track of where your children have been online and report back to you at regular intervals.

Some parents are adamant that it is their duty as good parents to spy on their children to make sure that they are safe. They install external controls to make sure that the children are not doing things that they are not supposed to. Other parents insist that they have access to all their children's passwords and check their browsing history every day to see what they have been up to online. They want to ensure that their children have not been accessing pornography or adult gaming sites amongst other inappropriate material.

Apart from being an exhausting exercise, I am not convinced that this practice is useful or effective in the long term. Installing external controls for children may keep them off certain sites in the short term, but when children are spied on, they often become more sneaky and learn to cover their tracks. Since the children are digital natives, they are likely to find a way around the controls quite quickly. So, while external monitoring by parents may prevent them from inappropriate behaviour for a short time, it is unlikely to be effective in the long run to help them make good decisions about their relationship with technology.

Constant surveillance, moreover, teaches them nothing more than to be on guard from parental eyes. However, it does not, in my opinion, teach them the skills of internal management and self-regulation. It does nothing to instil values or good decision-making. It is these skills that will eventually keep them safe online and in the real world and help them grow into thoughtful, aware young adults who are an asset to themselves and the community.

And yet, I am also realistic that in this day and age, the

Internet throws stuff at children that their young souls cannot handle. Some of it comes at them unasked for and unsearched. It is much too tempting for curious young minds to explore these links even as they are horrified by what they see and experience. For situations like this, spy software and controls on your computer definitely have a place. We must be cautious, however, that they do not replace the other work that we must do to prepare the Net Generation. Spy software will be damaging to our families if it gives us a false sense of comfort that our children are safe.

I hope that this book has cautioned you about the dangers inherent in today's world. More than that, I hope that it has given you a sense of your own power to positively influence your family and some tools to support you in this journey.

I wish you the very best on the exciting journey of parenthood. May the bumps on the road be few, the view spectacular and the ride mostly smooth!

References

Part 1: FACING REALITY

Chapter 1: Exploring the Digital Landscape

1. For example, Danah Boyd. 2014. *It's Complicated: The Social Lives of Networked Teens*. Yale: Yale University Press.
2. Sonia Livingstone, Leslie Haddon, Anke Görzig, and Kjartan Ólafsson. 2011. 'Risks and safety on the internet: the perspective of European children: full findings and policy implications from the EU Kids Online survey of 9–16 year olds and their parents in 25 countries'. EU Kids Online, Deliverable D4. EU Kids Online Network, London, UK, accessed February 2015, http://eprints.lse.ac.uk/33731/
3. Amanda Lenhart, Kristen Purcell, Aaron Smith, and Kathryn Zickuhr. 2010. 'Social Media & Mobile Internet Use Among Teens and Young Adults'. Washington, DC: Pew Internet & American Life Project.

Chapter 2: What Are Your Children Doing Online?

1. 'Parenting in the Age of Digital Technology'. 2013. Center on Media and Human Development at School of Communication, Northwestern University.
2. Ibid.
3. Ibid.
4. Jeffery Cole, PhD. 2013. 'The 2013 Digital Future Report'. USC Annenberg School Center for the Digital Future, University of Southern California.
5. Ibid.
6. Ibid.
7. Ibid.
8. Ibid.
9. M. Madden, S. Cortesi, U. Gasser, A. Lenhart, and M. Duggan.

2012. *Parents, Teens, and Online Privacy*. Washington DC: Pew Research Center.

10. Ibid.

11. Ibid.

12. 'Generation M2: Media in the Lives of 8- to 18-Year-Olds'. 20 January 2010. Menlow Park, California: Kaiser Family Foundation.

13. Ibid.

14. Andrew J. Flanagin, Mirim J. Metzger, and Ethan Hartsell. 2010. *Kids and Credibility: An Empirical Examination of Youth, Digital Media Use, and Information Credibility*. Cambridge MA: John D. and Catherine T. MacArthur Foundation Reports on Digital Media and Learning.

15. N. Ellison and J. Vitak. 2015. 'Social Network Site Affordances and their Relationship to Social Capital Processes' in S. Sundar, (ed.) *The Handbook of the Psychology of Communication Technology*. Hoboken, NJ: Wiley-Blackwell, pp. 205–27; N. Ellison, J. Vitak, R. Gray, and C. Lampe. 2014. 'Cultivating Social Resources on Social Network Sites: Facebook Relationship Maintenance Behaviors and Their Role in Social Capital Processes'. *Journal of Computer-Mediated Communication,* 19 (4): 855–70.

16. Juliana Menasce Horowitz. 2011. 'Global Digital Communication: Texting, Social Networking Popular Worldwide', Washington DC: Pew Research Center, Global attitudes project.

17. Norton Online Family. 2010. www.us.norton.com (The site also has downloadable reports for many countries, including India, China and Japan.)

18. Sonia Livingstone, Leslie Haddon, Görzig Anke and Kjartan Ólafsson. 2011. 'Risks and safety on the internet: the perspective of European children: full findings and policy implications from the EU Kids Online survey of 9–16 year olds and their parents in 25 countries'. EU Kids Online, Deliverable D4. London: EU Kids Online Network.

19. M. Madden and A. Lenhart. 2013. 'Teens, Social Media and Privacy'. Pew Internet and American Life Project, 21 May.

http://pewinternet.org/Reports/2013/Teens-Social-Media-And-Privacy.aspx.

20. Norton Online Family. 2010. www.us.norton.com
21. Elizabeth Stutz. 1996. 'Is Electronic Entertainment Hindering Children's Play and Social Development?' *Electronic Children: How Children are Responding to the Information Revolution*. Tim Gill (ed.). London: National Children's Bureau, pp. 59–70.
22. Ibid.
23. James Newman. 2004. *Videogames*. London: Routledge.
24. Roberto Bertolini and Simona Nissim. 2002. 'Video Games and Children's Imagination'. *Journal of Child Psychotherapy*, 28 (3): 305–25.

Part 2: ASSESSING THE IMPACT OF TECHNOLOGY

Chapter 3: Impact on the Brain

1. Kristen Purcell, Lee Rainie et al. 2012. 'How Teens Do Research in the Digital World', Washington DC: Pew Research Center Report.
2. Kristen Purcell, Lee Rainie et al. 2012. 'How Teens Do Research in the Digital World', Washington DC: Pew Research Center Report; Crista Sumanik. 2012. 'Entertainment Media Diets of Children and Adolescents May Impact Learning'. Common Sense Media Report.
3. 'Attention-Deficit / Hyperactivity Disorder (ADHD)'. http://www.cdc.gov/ncbddd/adhd/data.html
4. Dimitri A. Christakis, MD, MPH, Fredrick J. Zimmerman, PhD, David L. DeGiuseppe, and Carolyn A. MacCarty, PhD. 2004. 'Early Television Exposure and Subsequent Attentional Problems In Children'. *Pediatrics*, 113 (4): 708–15.
5. Ibid.
6. L. Rosen. 5 November 2014. 'ADHD and Technology: Helping Our Children Reclaim Their Focus and Attention'. http://www.huffingtonpost.com/dr-larry-rosen/adhd-and-technology-helpi_b_6096168.html

7. Mike Masnik. 2005. 'Technology Induced ADD?'. https://www.techdirt.com/articles/20050328/1051222.shtml

8. For example, K.S. Young. 2004. 'Internet Addiction: A New Clinical Phenomenon and Its Consequences'. *American Behavioral Scientist*, 48 (1): 402–15; and D. Roman. 2009. 'Internet Addition: It's Spreading, but is it Real?'. *Communications of the ACM*, 52 (12): 12.

9. Akamai and Gomez.com. 'Speed Is A Killer—Why Decreasing Page Load Time Can Drastically Increase Conversions'. https://blog. kissmetrics.com/speed-is-a-killer/.

10. Jakob Nielsen. 1997. 'How Users Read on the Web', Nielsen Norman Group. http://www.nngroup.com/articles/how-users-read-on-the-web/

11. Nicholas Carr. 2010. *The Shallows, What the Internet is Doing to our Brains*. New York: Norton; 'Is Google Making Us Stupid?' in Mark Bauerlein (ed.). 2011. *The Digital Divide: Arguments for and Against Facebook, Google, Texting, and the Age of Social Networking*. Tarcher.

12. 'How People Read on the Web: The Eyetracking Evidence', a study by the Nielsen Norman Group; J. Morkes and J. Nielsen. 1997. 'Concise, SCANNABLE, and Objective: How to Write for the Web'. http://www.nngroup.com/articles/how-users-read-on-the-web/ and http://www.nngroup.com/articles/concise-scannable-and-objective-how-to-write-for-the-web/

13. B. Cooper. 2013. '7 Powerful Facebook Statistics You Should Know About'. http://www.fastcompany.com/3022301/work-smart/7-powerful- facebook-statistics-you-should-know-about

14. Author Nicholas Larr: The Web shatters forms, rewires brains http://www.wired.com/2010/05/ff_nicholas_carr/

15. Ellen Galinsky. 2010. *Mind in the Making: The Seven Essential Life Skills Every Child Needs*. New York: William Morrow Paperbacks.

16. James Marshall, PhD. 2002. 'Learning with Technology: Evidence that can and does support Learning', White Paper published by San Diego State University. http://www.dcmp.org/caai/nadh176.pdf

17. T.A. Pempek, L.B. Demers, K. Hanso, H.L. Kirkorian, et al. 2011. 'The impact of baby videos on parent–child interaction'. *Journal of Applied Developmental Psychology*. 32: 10–19; M.L. Courage and A.E. Setliff. 2010. 'When babies watch television: Attention-getting, attention-holding, and The implications for learning from video material'. *Developmental Review*. 30: 220–38; and Dimitri A. Christakis. 2009. 'The effects of infant media usage: what do we know and what should we learn?' *Acta Pædiatrica*. 98: 8–16.

18. Stuart Wolport. 2009. 'Is technology producing a decline in critical thinking and analysis? Studies shed light on multi-tasking, video games and learning', UCLA Newsroom communication.

19. C.B. Fried. 2007. 'In-class laptop use and its effects on student learning'. *Computers & Education*. doi:10.1016/j.compedu. 2006.09.006.

20. A. Gorlick. 2009. 'Media multitaskers pay mental price, Stanford study shows'. http://news.stanford.edu/news/2009/august24/ multitask-research-study-082409.html

21. Eyal Ophir, Clifford Nass and Anthony D. Wagner. 2009. 'Cognitive control in media multitaskers'. *Proceedings of the National Academy of Sciences*, September. 106 (37): 15583–7. DOI:10.1073/pnas.0903620106.

22. Rebecca Clay. 2009. 'Mini-multitaskers: For young people, a tendency to multitask may impoverish learning, productivity and even friendships'. *American Psychological Association*, 40 (2).

23. Adam Gorlick. 2009. 'Media multitaskers pay mental price', Stanford Report, 24 August.

24. M. Richtel. 2010. 'Growing Up Digital, Wired for Distraction'. http://www.nytimes.com/2010/11/21/technology/21 brain.html?pagewanted=all.&_r=0

25. Mihály Csikszentmihályi. 2008. *Flow: The Psychology of Optimal Experience*. USA: Harper & Row.

26. 'Interruption Science: Costly Distractions at Work'. 2005. 14 October, http://www.npr.org/templates/story/story.php?storyId= 4958831

27. G. Mark, V. Gonzalez, and J. Harris. 2005. 'No Task Left Behind? Examining the Nature of Fragmented Work'. *Proceedings of CHI'05*, 113–20.

28. Stuart Wolport. 2009. 'Is technology producing a decline in critical thinking and analysis? Studies shed light on multitasking, video games and learning', UCLA Newsroom communication.

Chapter 4: Impact on Health and Physical Development

1. Centre for Disease Control (CDC) report. http://www.cdc.gov/pdf/facts_about_obesity_in_the_united_states.pdf

2. 'Global, regional, and national prevalence of overweight and obesity in children and adults during 1980–2013: a systematic analysis for the Global Burden of Disease Study'. 2013. Institute for Health Metrics and Evaluation.http://www.healthdata.org/research-article/global-regional-and-national-prevalence overweight-and-obesity-children-and-adults

3. V. Rideout. 2011. *Zero to eight: Children's media use in America*. San Francisco, CA: Commonsense Media. (Further analysis of original data published by Commonsense Media was conducted on 4 October 2012 by Melissa Saphir and Vicky Rideout at the request of this publication.)

4. Dr Pradeep K. Chowbey. 25 May 2012. 'Big isn't beautiful: From a cosmetic problem, obesity is now a bonafide disease'. *India Today*. http://indiatoday.intoday.in/story/health-special-2012-pradeep-k-chowbey-obesity-surgery/1/197548.html

5. Andrea Cespedes. 2013. 'Obesity in Children & Technology'. http://www.livestrong.com/article/46320-obesity-children-technology/

6. Centre for Disease Control and Prevention (CDC) Report: Physical Activity Facts. http://www.cdc.gov/healthyschools/physicalactivity/facts.htm

7. R.H. Jacobs, E.G. Becker-Weidman, M.A. Reinecke, N. Jordan, S.G.Silva, P. Rohde, J.S. March. 2010. 'Treating depression and oppositional behavior in adolescents'. *Journal of Clinical Child and Adolescent Psychology*. January, 39 (4): 559–67.

8. American College of Sports Medicine Brochure. https://www.acsm.org/docs/brochures/exergaming.pdf?sfvrsn=6

9. 'Technology is "a back injury time bomb" for children'. 2013. http://www.telegraph.co.uk/news/health/news/10445315/Technology-is-a-back-injury-time-bomb-for-children.html

10. N. Gaudin. 2011. 'IARC classifies radiofrequency electromagnetic fields as possibly carcinogenic to humans'. http://www.iarc.fr/en/media-centre/pr/2011/pdfs/pr208_E.pdf

11. Lennart Hardell, Michael Carlberg, Fredrik Söderqvist, Kjell Hansson Mild, and L. Lloyd Morgan. September 2007. 'Long-term use of cellular phones and brain tumours: increased risk associated with use for 10 years'. *Occupational and Environmental Medicine.* 64 (9): 626–32.

12. R. Cohen. 2014. 'Are wireless phones linked with brain cancer risk?'. http://www.reuters.com/article/us-brain-cancer-mobile phoneidUSKCN0IV26Y20141111#qk8kREEpoQdb WKgd.97

13. Parliamentary Assembly, Council of Europe. 27 May 2011. 'The potential dangers of electromagnetic fields and their effect on the environment'. Committee on the Environment, Agriculture and Local and Regional Affairs. http://assembly.coe.int/nw/xml/XRef/Xref-XML2HTML-en.asp?fileid=17994&

14. 'International Warnings on Wi-Fi and Microwave Radiation'. 2011. http://www.safeinschool.org/2011/01/international-warnings-on-wi-fi.html

15. Parliamentary Assembly, Council of Europe. 27 May 2011. 'The potential dangers of electromagnetic fields and their effect on the environment'. Committee on the Environment, Agriculture and Local and Regional Affairs. http://assembly.coe.int/nw/xml/XRef/Xref-XML2HTML-en.asp?fileid=17994&

16. C. Rowan. 2009. 'Technology overuse on child sensory development'. http://www.zoneinworkshops.com/pdf/Summer2009-OTLine-Technology-overuse-on-child-sensory-development.pdf

17. Nicole Bogart. 5 February 2014 'Kids learning digital skills before life skills'. *Globe and Mail*, Toronto.

18. AVG Digital Diaries. 2014. http://www.avg.com/digitaldiaries/ 2014

19. 'Sleep In America Poll Finds Children Sleep Better When Parents Establish Rules, Limit Technology and Set a Good Example'. 2014. National Sleep Foundation News Release.

20. Kaiser Family Foundation. 2008. 'Children's Media Use and Sleep Problems: Issues and Unanswered Questions'. http://kff.org/ other/issue-brief/childrens-media-use-and-sleep-problems-issues/.

21. 'Physical Activity In Children Improves Their Sleeping Patterns'. 2009. *Medical News Today*. http://www.medical newstoday.com/articles/158482.php

22. F. Willick. 2013. 'Study delves into dark corners of kids and sleep deprivation'. http://thechronicleherald.ca/novascotia/ 1167418-study-delves-into-dark-corners-of-kids-and-sleep-deprivation

Chapter 5: Faking It on Facebook: Impact on Self-image

1. Mark A. Urista, Qingwen Dong, and Kenneth D. Day. 2008. 'Explaining Why Young Adults Use MySpace and Facebook Through Uses and Gratifications Theory'. *Human Communication*, a publication of the Pacific and Asian Communication Association. 12 (2): 215–29.

2. Richard M. Lerner and M. Ann Easterbrooks. 2003. *Developmental Psychology*, vol. 6 of Irving B. Weiner, Donald K. Freedheim (eds). *Handbook of Psychology*. New Jersey: Wiley.

3. Mark T. Greenberg, Judith M. Siegel, and Cynthia J. Leitch. 1983. 'The nature and importance of attachment relationships to parents and peers during adolescence'. *Journal of Youth and Adolescence*, October, 12 (5): 373–86.

4. J.T. Hancock and C. Toma. 2013. 'Self-affirmation underlies Facebook use'. *Personality and Social Psychology Bulletin*. 39: 321–31.

5. Ibid.

6. S. Zarghooni. 2007. 'A study of self-presentation in light of Facebook'. Institute of Psychology, University of Oslo. http://

folk.uio.no/sasanz/ academic%20work/Selfpresentation_on_Facebook.pdf.

7. Theodora Stites. 2006. 'Modern Love: Someone to Watch Over Me (on a Google Map)'. *New York Times*, 9 July. http://www.nytimes.com/2006/07/09/fashion/sundaystyles/09love.html?_r=0

8. A.L. Forest and J.V. Wood. 2011. 'When social networking is not working: Individuals with low self-esteem recognize but do not reap the benefits of self-disclosure on Facebook'. *Psychological Science,* 23: 295–302.

9. J. Nie and S.S. Sundar. 2013. 'Who Would Pay for Facebook? Self Esteem as a Predictor of User Behavior, Identity Construction and Valuation of Virtual Possessions', in P. Kotzé et al. (eds), *Proceedings of INTERACT 2013, Part III, LNCS 8119*, pp. 726–43.

10. Amy L. Gonzales. and Jeffrey T. Hancock, PhD. 2011. 'Mirror, Mirror on my Facebook Wall: Effects of Exposure to Facebook on Self-Esteem'. *Cyberpsychology, Behavior, and Social Networking*, 14 (1–2).

11. Amanda L. Forest and Joanne V. Wood. 2012. 'When Social Networking Is Not Working: Individuals With Low Self-Esteem Recognize but Do Not Reap the Benefits of Self-Disclosure on Facebook'. *Psychological Science*, March, 23 (3): 295–302.

12. A. Oeldorf-Hirsch and S.S. Sundar. 2015. 'Posting, commenting, and tagging: Effects of sharing news stories on Facebook'. *Computers in Human Behavior*, 44: 240–49.

13. Soraya Mehdizadeh. 2010. 'Self-Presentation 2.0: Narcissism and Self-Esteem on Facebook'. *Cyberpsychology, Behavior, and Social Networking*. August, 13 (4): 357–64. doi:10.1089/cyber.2009.0257.

14. Moira Burke, Cameron Marlow, and Thomas Lento. 2010. 'Social Network Activity and Social Well-Being', *CHI 2010*, Atlanta, Georgia, USA.

15. S. Turkle. 2011. 'Alone Together: Why we expect more from technology and less from each other'. New York: Basic Books.

16. Angie Zuo. 2014–15. 'Measuring Up: Social Comparisons on Facebook and Contributions to Self-Esteem and Mental Health'.

17. A.H. Jordan, B. Monin, C.S. Dweck, B.J. Lovett, O.P. John, J.J. Gross. 2011. 'Misery has more company than people think: underestimating the prevalence of others' negative emotions'. Personality and Social Psychology Bulletin. January, 37 (1): 120–35. doi: 10.1177/0146167210390822.

18. Ibid.

19. 'Body Image Friend or Foe? How is Facebook affecting the way you feel about your Body?' 2012. The Center for Eating Disorders Blog. http://eatingdisorder.org/blog/2012/03/body-image-friend-or-foe-how-is-facebook-affecting-the-way-you-feel-about-your-body/

20. Ibid.

21. E. Kross, P. Verduyn, E. Demiralp, J. Park, D.S. Lee, et al. 2013. 'Facebook Use Predicts Declines in Subjective Well-Being in Young Adults'. Public Library of Science (PLoS ONE), 8 (8). e69841. doi:10.1371/journal.pone.0069841.

22. Laura Donnelly. 2012. 'Facebook and Twitter feed anxiety, study finds'. http://www.telegraph.co.uk/technology/9383609/Facebook-and-Twitter-feed-anxiety-study-finds.html

23. Mark Bauerlein (ed). 2001. *The Digital Divide: Arguments for and Against Facebook, Google, Texting, and the Age of Social Networking*. New York: Penguin.

24. D. Brooks. 2011. 'The Saga of Sister Kiki' *The New York Times*. http://www.nytimes.com/2011/06/24/opinion/24brooks.html

Chapter 6: Impact on Relationships and Communication

1. For example, *Archives of General Psychiatry,* December 2005. WebMD Health News: 'For Happiness, Seek Family, Not Fortune'.

2. Seminar in Communication Studies, California State University, Northridge. http://hyper.vcsun.org/HyperNews/battias/get/cs600/talk/18.html?nogifs; Allan Canfield, PhD. 2002. 'Body, Identity and Interaction: Interpreting Non-verbal Communication'. http://canfield.etext.net/index.htm

3. For example, Tom R. Tyler. 2002. 'Is the Internet Changing Social Life? It seems the more the things change, the more they stay the same'. *Journal of Social Issues.* 58 (1): 195–205; S. Turkle. 2011. 'Alone Together: Why we expect more from technology and less from each other'. New York: Basic Books.

4. The Kaiser Foundation. 20 January 2010. 'Daily Media Use Among Children and Teens Up Dramatically From Five Years Ago'. http://kff.org/disparities-policy/press-release/daily-media-use-among-children-and-teens-up-dramatically-from-five-years-ago/

5. P. Gottman.1997. *Raising the Emotionally Intelligent Child.* New York: Simon & Schuster.

6. Kari Henley. 2009. 'Are Facebook Friends "Real" Friends?'. http://www.huffingtonpost.com/kari-henley/are-facebook-friends-real_b_180204.html

7. Pamela Paul. 19 December 2014. 'How to Be Liked by Everyone Online'. *New York Times.*

8. Kaveri Subrahmanyam and Patricia Greenfield. 2008. 'Communicating Online: Adolescent Relationships and the Media'. *The Future of Children.* 18 (1).

9. R.I.M. Dunbar, 1992. 'Neocortex size as a constraint on group size in primates'. *Journal of Human Evolution.* 22 (6): 469–93.

10. Matthew E. Brashears. 2011. 'Small networks and high isolation?: A reexamination of American discussion networks'. *Social Networks,* 33 (4): 331–41.

11. Ibid.

12. Theodora Stites. 2006. 'Modern Love: Someone to Watch Over Me (on a Google Map)'. *New York Times,* 9 July. http://www.nytimes.com/2006/07/09/fashion/sundaystyles/09love.html?_r=0

13. Amanda Lenhart. 2012. 'Teens, Smartphones and Texting: Texting Volume is up While the Frequency of Voice Calling is Down. About one in four teens say they own smartphones'. Pew Research Center's Internet and American Life Project, 19 March. http://pewinternet.org/Reports/2012/Teens-and-smartphones.aspx.

14. Kaveri Subrahmanyam and Patricia Greenfield. 2008. 'Communicating Online: Adolescent Relationships and the Media'. *The Future of Children*. 18 (1).

15. Sara H. Konrath, Edward H. O'Brien, and Courtney Hsing. 2011. 'Changes in Dispositional Empathy in American College Students Over Time: A Meta-Analysis'. *Personality and Social Psychology Review*, pp. 180–98.

Chapter 7: Impact on the Soul

1. T. Nudd. 6 November 2009. 'Rihanna gives painful details of Chris Brown assault'. *CNN*. http://edition.cnn.com/2009/SHOWBIZ/Music/11/06/rihanna.chris.brown/index.html?eref=ib_us

2. Reg Bailey. 2011. 'Letting Children be Children. Report of an Independent Review of the Commercialisation and Sexualisation of Childhood'. Presented to the UK Parliament by the Secretary of State for Education by Command of Her Majesty.

3. Ibid.

4. Jane D. Brown and Kelly L. L'Engle. 2009. 'X-Rated: Sexual Attitudes and Behaviors Associated With US Early Adolescents' Exposure to Sexually Explicit Media'. *Communication Research*. 36 (1): 129–51.

5. Ibid.

6. J. Brown, K. L'Engle, C. Pardun, G. Guo, K. Kenneavy, and C. Jackson. 2006. 'Sexy media matter: Exposure to sexual content in music, movies, television and magazines predicts black and white adolescents' sexual behavior'. *Pediatrics,* 117: 1018-1027.

7. R. Collins, M. Elliott, S. Berry, D. Kanouse, D. Kunkel, S. Hunter, et al. 2004. 'Watching sex on television predicts adolescent initiation of sexual behavior'. *Pediatrics,* 114 (3): E280-E289.

8. S. Escobar-Chaves, S. Tortolero, C. Markham, B. Low, P. Eitel, and P. Thickstun. 2005. 'Impact of the media on adolescent sexual attitudes and behaviors'. *Pediatrics,* 116 (1): 303–26; S. Fineran and L. Bennett. 1999. 'Gender and power issues of

sexual harassment among teenagers'. *Journal of Interpersonal Violence*, 14 (6): 626–41.

9. Y.T. Uhls and P.M. Greenfield. 2011. 'The Rise of Fame: An Historical Content Analysis'. *Cyberpsychology: Journal of Psychosocial Research on Cyberspace.* 5 (1), article 1; Y.T. Uhls, E. Zgourou, and P. Greenfield. 2014. '21st century media, fame, and other future aspirations: A national survey of 9–15 year olds'. *Cyberpsychology: Journal of Psychosocial Research on Cyberspace.* 8 (4), article 5.

10. Y.T. Uhls and P.M. Greenfield. 2011. 'The Rise of Fame: An Historical Content Analysis'. *Cyberpsychology: Journal of Psychosocial Research on Cyberspace.* 5 (1), article 1.

11. Dimitri A. Christakis, MD, MPH, Frederick J. Zimmerman, PhD., David L. DiGiuseppe, and Carolyn A. McCarty. 2004. 'Early Television Exposure and Subsequent Attentional Problems in Children'. *Pediatrics*, 113 (4): 708–15.

12. B. Pytel. 2007. 'Cheating is on the rise: Surveys shows less integrity among high school and college students'. www.suite101.com/content/cheating-is-on-the-rise-a31238

13. Teenage Sexting Statistics. http://www.guardchild.com/teenage-sexting-statistics/

14. Ibid.

15. Amanda Lenhart. 15 December 2009. 'Teens and Sexting'. Pew Research Center. http://www.pewinternet.org/2009/12/15/teens-and-sexting/

16. CNN Report. 2009. '"Sexting" lands teen on sex offender list', 8 April. http://edition.cnn.com/2009/CRIME/04/07/sexting.busts/.

17. B. Gallagher. 9 September 2013. 'Snapchat Now Sees 350M Photos Shared Daily, Up From 200M in June'. *Tech Crunch.* http://techcrunch.com/2013/09/09/snapchat-now-sees-350m-photos-shared-daily-up-from-200m-in-june/

18. Eugene V. Beresin, MD. 2009. *The Impact of Media Violence on Children and Adolescents: Opportunities for Clinical Interventions.* American Academy of Child and Adolescent Psychiatry.

19. Eric W. Owens, Richard J. Behun, Jill C. Manning, and Rory C.

Reid. 2012. 'The Impact of Internet Pornography on Adolescents: A Review of the Research'. *Sexual Addiction & Compulsivity*. 19: 99–122; Tracy L. Tylka. 2015. 'No harm in looking, right? Men's pornography consumption, body image, and well-being'. *Psychology of Men & Masculinity*. January,16 (1): 97–107. http://dx.doi.org/10.1037/a0035774.

20. Dimitri A. Christakis, MD, MPH, Frederick J. Zimmerman, PhD, David L. DeGiuseppe, and Carolyn A. MacCarty, PhD. 2004. 'Early Television Exposure and Subsequent Attentional Problems In Children'. *Pediatrics*, 113 (4): 708–15.

21. Brad J. Bushman, PhD, L. Rowell Huesmann, PhD. 2006. 'Short-term and Long-term Effects of Violent Media on Aggression in Children and Adults'. *Archives of Pediatric and Adolescent Medicine*.160 (4): 348–52. doi:10.1001/archpedi.160.4.348.

22. L. Miller. 1995. 'Tough guys: Psychotherapeutic strategies with law enforcement and emergency services personnel'. *Psychotherapy*, 32: 592–600.

23. Michele Cooley-Strickland, Tanya J. Quille, Robert S. Griffin, Elizabeth A. Stuart, Catherine P. Bradshaw, and Debra Furr-Holden. 2009. 'Community Violence and Youth: Affect, Behavior, Substance Use, and Academics'. *Clinical Child Family Psychology Review*. 12 (2): 127–56. doi: 10.1007/s10567-009-0051-6.

24. Policy Statement from the American Academy of Pediatrics. 2009. 'Children, Adolescents, and the Media'. *Pediatrics*. 132 (5). 1 November 2009, 958–61. doi: 10.1542/peds.2013-2656.

25. David Brooks. 2011. 'The Saga of Sister Kiki'. Opinion Page, *New York Times*. http://www.nytimes.com/2011/06/24/opinion/24brooks.html

Part 3: STEPS TO THRIVING AS A FAMILY IN THE DIGITAL AGE

Chapter 8: Danger and Safety in Cyberspace

1. Bob Sullivan. 2015. 'What you don't know can hurt your kids'. Security on NBC News. http://www.nbcnews.com/id/3078811/

ns/technology_and_science-security/t/what-you-dont-know-can-hurt-kids/

2. J. Wolak, K. Mitchell, and D. Finkelhor. 2006. 'Online Victimization of Youth: Five Years Later'. Alexandria, VA: National Center for Missing and Exploited Children.

3. Kimberly J. Mitchell, David Finkelhor, Lisa M. Jones, Janis Wolak. 2010. 'Use of Social Networking Sites in Online Sex Crimes Against Minors: An Examination of National Incidence and Means of Utilization'. *Journal of Adolescent Health* 47. August 2010, Volume 47, Issue 2, Pages 183–190.

4. Cyber Bullying [def](n.d.). US Legal Dictionary, USLegal.com. http://definitions.uslegal.com/c/cyber-bullying/

5. E. Pilkington. 30 September 2010. 'Tyler Clementi, student outed as gay on internet, jumps to his death'. *The Guardian*, UK. http://www.theguardian.com/world/2010/sep/30/tyler-clementi-gay-student-suicide

6. Helen Cowie. 2013. 'Cyberbullying and its impact on young people's emotional health and well-being'. *The Psychiatrist*, 37 (5).

7. Sameer Hinduja, PhD and Justin W. Patchin, PhD. 2007. 'Offline consequences of online victimization: School violence and delinquency'. *Journal of School Violence*, 6(3), 89112.

8. V. Šleglova and A. Cerna. 2011. 'Cyberbullying in Adolescent Victims: Perception and Coping'. *Cyberpsychology: Journal of Psychosocial Research on Cyberspace,* 5 (2). http://cyberpsychology.eu/view.php?cisloclanku=2011121901&article=1.

9. Cyber Bullying: Statistics and Tips (n.d). I Safe.org. https://www.isafe.org/outreach/media/media_cyber_bullying

10. Cyber Bullying Statistics (n.d). Bullying Statistics.com. http://www.bullyingstatistics.org/content/cyber-bullying-statistics.html

11. Cyber Bullying: Statistics and Tips (n.d). I Safe.org. https://www.isafe.org/outreach/media/media_cyber_bullying

12. Ibid.

13. Ibid.

14. Julian Dooley, Jacek Pyzalski, and Donna Cross. 2009.

'Cyberbullying Versus Face-to-Face Bullying: A Theoretical and Conceptual Review'. *Journal of Psychology*, 217 (4):182–88.

15. Ibid.

16. 'If You Have Something You Don't Want Anyone To Know, Maybe You Shouldn't Be Doing It'. 18 March 2010. *The Huffington Post*. http://www.huffingtonpost.com/2009/12/07/google-ceo-on-privacy-if_n_383105.html?

17. S. Dredge. 13 November 2013. 'Ten things you need to know about Snapchat'. *The Guardian*. http://www.theguardian.com/technology/2013/nov/13/snapchat-app-sexting-lawsuits-valuation

18. Sara A. Wright. 2008. 'Blinding Lights: The Negative Effects of the Media on Celebrities'. San Luis Obispo: Journalism Department California Polytechnic State University.

19. 'Research finds 94% of UK parents have posted photos of their kids online'. 27 August 2013. Breaking News.ie. http://www.breakingnews.ie/world/research-finds-94-of-uk-parents-have-posted-photos-of-their-kids-online-604911.html

20. B. Williams. 2013. 'NZ's ever growing digital footprint'. 24 February. http://www.nurve.co.nz/our-blog/87-nzs-growing-digital-footprint

21. D. Holloway, L. Green, and S. Livingstone. 2013. *Zero to eight: Young children and their internet use.* London School of Economics, London: EU Kids Online.

22. Kate Mackenzie. 2006. 'Encouraging information sharing'. *Financial Times*, 24 January.

23. Frank W. Abagnale. 2008. *Stealing Your Life: The Ultimate Identity Theft Prevention Plan.* New York: Broadway Books.

Chapter 9: Step 1: Get Your Own Act Together

1. Albert Bandura.1971. *Social Learning Theory.* New York: General Learning Press.

2. H. Rich and T. Barker. 2002. *In the Moment: Celebrating the Everyday.* New York: Harper Collins; S. Dominus. 2010. 'A Facebook Movement against Mom and Dad'. *New York Times*, 16 January; B. Worthen. 29 September 2012. 'The Perils of Texting While Parenting'. *Wall Street Journal*.

3. Sean Elder. 27 July 2014. 'A Korean Couple Let a Baby Die While They Played a Video Game'. *Newsweek.*

4. Andrew Salmon. 2 April 2010. 'Couple: Internet Gaming Addiction Led to Baby's Death'. *CNN.* http://edition.cnn.com/2010/WORLD/asiapcf/04/01/korea.parents.starved.baby/

5. B. Worthen. 29 September 2012. 'The Perils of Texting While Parenting'. *Wall Street Journal.*

6. Michael Lamport Commons and Patrice Marie Miller. 2015. 'The benefits of attachment parenting for infants and children: A behavioral developmental view'. *Behavioral Development Bulletin,* 01/2015, 10 (1): 1–14. doi: 10.1037/h0100514.

7. H.J. Polan and M.J. Ward. October 1994. 'Role of the mother's touch in failure to thrive: a preliminary investigation'. *Journal of the American Academy of Child & Adolescent Psychiatry,* 33 (8).

8. 'Can holding, cuddling, and eye contact help babies grow and develop?' Zero to Three, National Center for Infants, Toddlers and Families. http://www.zerotothree.org/child-development/school-readiness/qa/can-holding-cuddling-and-eye-contact-help-babies-grow-and-develop.html

9. Mark T. Greenberg, Dante Cicchetti, E. Mark Cummings. 1990. *Attachment in the Preschool Years: Theory, Research, and Intervention.* Chicago: University of Chicago Press.

10. Jenny S. Radesky, Caroline J. Kistin, Barry Zuckerman, Katie Nitzberg, Jamie Gross, Margot Kaplan-Sanoff, Marilyn Augustyn, and Michael Silverstein. 2014. 'Patterns of Mobile Device Use by Caregivers and Children During Meals in Fast Food Restaurants'. *Pediatrics,* April, 133 (4). http://pediatrics.aappublications.org/content/pediatrics/133/4/e843.full.pdf

11. 'The State of the Kid Survey'. 2014. *Highlights Magazine.* https://www.highlights.com/state-of-the-kid

12. 'Friends, Following and Feedback. How we are using social media'. 2011. http://www.nielsen.com/us/en/insights/news/2011/friends-following-and-feedback-how-were-using-social-media.html

13. Martha Anne Kitzrow. 2003. 'The Mental Health Needs of

Today's College Students: Challenges and Recommendations'. Fall. *NASPA Journal*, 41 (1).

14. Alana Klein. 2010. 'Incoming college students rate emotional health at record low, annual survey finds'. The American Freshman: National Norms for Fall. *Higher Education Research Institute Press Release*. http://heri.ucla.edu/pr-display.php?prQry=%2055

15. Ibid.

16. 'College students' mental health is a growing concern, survey finds'. 2013. June, 44 (6). American Psychological Association News Brief. http://www.apa.org/monitor/2013/06/college-students.aspx

17. Ron Taffel. 2009. *Childhood Unbound: Saving Our Kids' Best Selves—Confident Parenting in a World of Change*. New York: Free Press.

18. Ibid.

19. Ibid.

20. 'State of the Kid Survey'. 2014. *Highlights Magazine*. https://www.highlights.com/state-of-the-kid

21. 'Children and Parents: Media Use and Attitudes Report'. 2014. http://stakeholders.ofcom.org.uk/binaries/research/media-literacy/media-use-attitudes-14/Childrens_2014_Report.pdf.

22. 'Jam Kotenko Facebook identity fraud is up and you need to be careful'. 2013. 30 August 30, Digital Trends. http://www.digitaltrends.com/social-media/if-youre-not-careful-you-could-be-the-next-victim-of-identity-fraud-on-facebook/#ixzz3ZwslCxlz

23. Ibid.

24. 'Ex-conman Frank Abagnale warns how Facebook users risk identity theft'. 2013. http://www.theguardian.com/media/video/2013/mar/20/frank-abagnale-facebook-identity-theft-warning

25. Ibid.

26. Martin Robinson. 'British parents discover photos of their children have been stolen from Facebook and posted on a Russian website used by paedophiles'. 2015. *Daily Mail*, 13 January. http://

www.dailymail.co.uk/news/article-2908086/British-parents-discover-photos-children-stolen-Facebook-posted-Russian-website-used-paedophiles.html#ixzz3ZwuIXQaW

27. 'How to Identify a Target Market and Prepare a Customer Profile' (n.d). Edward Lowe Foundation. http://edwardlowe.org/digital-library/how-to-identify-a-target-market-and-prepare-a-customer-profile/

28. A. Marwick. 2013. 'Big Data, Data-Mining, and the Social Web. Governments, Corporations and Hackers: the Internet and Threats to the Privacy and Dignity of the Citizen. Power, Privacy and the Internet'. 2013. New York Review of Books conference, 30–31 October. New York: Scandinavia House.

Chapter 10: Step 2: Build a Relationship with Your Children

1. Daniel J. Kindlon. 2003. *Too Much of a Good Thing: Raising Children of Character in an Indulgent Age*. New York: Miramax Books.

2. Ibid.

3. Catherine Steiner-Adair. 2003. *The Big Disconnect: Protecting Childhood and Family Relationships in the Digital Age*. New York: HarperCollins.

4. David Popenoe. 1998. 'We Are What We See: The Family Conditions for Modeling Values for Children'. http://parenthood.library.wisc.edu/Popenoe/Popenoe-Modeling.html#ref1.

5. 'Can holding, cuddling, and eye contact help babies grow and develop?' Zero to Three, National Center for Infants, Toddlers and Families. http://www.zerotothree.org/child-development/school-readiness/qa/can-holding-cuddling-and-eye-contact-help-babies-grow-and-develop.html

6. Ibid.

7. Sarah Allen and Kerry Daly. 2007. 'The Effects of Father Involvement: An updated research summary of evidence inventory'. Centre for Families, Work & Well-Being, University of Guelph.

8. Miriam Weinstein. 2006. *The Surprising Power of Family Meals. How Eating Together Makes Us Smarter, Stronger, Healthier and Happier*. New York: Steerforth Press.

9. Ibid.

10. Ibid.

11. S.D. Whiteman and C.M.Buchanan. 2002. 'Mother's and children's expectations for adolescence: The impact of perceptions of an older sibling's experience'. *Journal of Family Psychology*, 16: 157–71.

Chapter 12: Step 4: Set Limits

1. Nick Bilton. 2014. 'Steve Jobs Was a Low-Tech Parent'. *New York Times*, 10 September. http://www.nytimes.com/2014/09/11/fashion/steve-jobs-apple-was-a-low-tech-parent.html

2. Ibid.

3. D. Holloway, L. Green, and S. Livingstone. 2013. *Zero to eight: Young children and their internet use*. LSE, London: EU Kids Online.

4. Ibid.

5. Dr Larry Rosen. 2014. 'ADHD and Technology: Helping Our Children Reclaim Their Focus and Attention'. *Huffington Post*, 11 May.

6. Ibid.

Chapter 13: Step 5: Build a Community of Support

1. Ron Taffel. 2009. *Childhood Unbound: Saving Our Kids' Best Selves: Confident Parenting in a World of Change*. New York: Free Press.

2. Robert Grimm, Kimberly Spring, and Nathan Dietz. 2007. *The Health Benefits of Volunteering: A Review of Recent Research*. Washington DC: Corporation for National and Community Service, Office of Research and Policy Development.

3. Daniel J. Kindlon. 2003. *Too Much of a Good Thing: Raising Children of Character in an Indulgent Age*. New York: Miramax Books.

69069032R00108

Made in the USA
Middletown, DE
04 April 2018